Magic
and
Misery

In memory of my Father,
John Hancock, who told me
my First stories.

Darby Creek
A division of Lerner Publishing Group, Inc.
241 First Avenue North
Minneapolis, MN 55401 USA

For reading levels and more information, look up this title at
www.lernerbooks.com.

Main body text set in Sabon LT Std 13/19.
Typeface provided by Adobe Systems.

Library of Congress Cataloging-in-Publication Data

Names: Pearson, Maggie, 1941– author. | Greenwood, Francesca, illustrator.
Title: Magic and misery : traditional tales from around the world / by Maggie
    Pearson ; illustrations by Francesca Greenwood.
Description: Minneapolis : Darby Creek, 2016. | Series: World of stories
Identifiers: LCCN 2015046660 (print) | LCCN 2016006992 (ebook) | ISBN
    9781512413199 (lb : alk. paper) | ISBN 9781512413410 (pb : alk. paper) |
    ISBN 9781512413427 (eb pdf)
Subjects: LCSH: Tales—Juvenile literature. | Legends—Juvenile literature.
Classification: LCC GR74 .P43 2016 (print) | LCC GR74 (ebook) | DDC
    398.2—dc23

LC record available at http://lccn.loc.gov/2015046660

Manufactured in the United States of America
1-39778-21316-3/3/2016

WORLD of STORIES

Magic
and
Misery

TRADITIONAL TALES FROM
AROUND THE WORLD

MAGGIE PEARSON

Illustrated by
Francesca Greenwood

MINNEAPOLIS

Contents

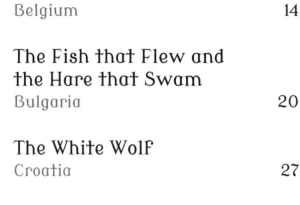

The Soldier's Bride
Austria

He was a soldier and she was his sweetheart. They promised to love each other till death and beyond. Then off he went to fight in the emperor's wars.

"I'll come back for you," he promised, "just as soon as I've made my fortune, and we'll find a place where we can be together always."

She waited and waited but he didn't come and he didn't write.

 9

So she crept down to the charnel house and she stole a dead man's skull. She put it in a pan of water, tossed in a handful of millet, and set it on the stove to simmer.

As midnight struck, the water began to bubble and boil.

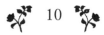

The skull bobbed up to the surface and three times it spoke.

The first time, "He is coming," it said.

The second time, "He is on his way."

The third time, "He is here, outside your door!"

She went to the door and opened it and there was her lover, seated on a horse as black as midnight.

"I have kept my promise," he said. "I have come for you. Do you still love me?" he asked her.

"I do!" she said. "Till death and beyond. So, have you made your fortune and have you found a place for us?"

"I have," he said. "I've found a place where we can be together always. Mount up behind me and I'll take you there."

So up she got and away they went, no sound but the horse's hooves on the darkling road, no light but a sliver of light from the new moon, thin as a miser's smile.

On they went and on again until they came to a graveyard and a new grave freshly dug.

"This is it," said her soldier lover, helping her down from the horse beside it. "This is our new home, where we can be together always."

Poor girl! She did still love him and she always would, till death and beyond, but she wasn't about to be buried alive.

"In you get," he said.

"You go first," she said. "Then you can help me down."

So in he got, into that freshly dug grave, but when he turned to help her down—she was away and running as if all the fiends of hell were at her heels!

Out of the churchyard and off down the road she ran, the sound of his footsteps pounding behind her. (Luckily he'd left the horse behind or she'd have stood no chance at all.)

On she ran, through the still, dark night

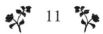 11

with her dead lover pounding after her. Not a creature stirring, not a mortal soul to help her, not a house where she could go for help.

Step by step he was gaining on her, the sound of his boots on the dark road coming nearer, nearer, and her own body growing—oh!—so weary, weary almost to death, when at last she spied a light in the distance.

So on she went and on again till she came to a house where the door stood open and in she ran, down a long, dark passageway to where the light was shining in a little, low, windowless room at the other end.

She slammed the door shut behind her and turned the key—not a moment too soon!

"Let me in!" cried the soldier, hammering on the door.

And a voice from behind her answered him, "Who calls?"

Looking around, she saw that the light she'd run toward came from four candles standing around a coffin. In the coffin lay a dead man with his eyes wide open.

"Who calls?" cried the dead man.

"One of your own kind," answered the soldier. "Brother, let me in."

"Brother, I will!" Slowly the dead man raised himself up in his coffin and the girl was thinking her last hour had surely come when from somewhere outside she heard the sound of a cock crowing to greet the morning sun.

At which the dead man lifted up his head, then lay down in his coffin again, and the hammering on the door was suddenly stilled.

When the people of the house broke down the door they thought at first it was an old, old woman they found there, crouched, sobbing and shivering, in the corner, for her hair had turned quite white.

The Traveler
From Paradise

Belgium

There was an old woman who had been widowed once and married twice.

One day, while her second husband was out working on the farm, a traveling man came knocking at the door in search of a bite to eat. So she gave him a bit of bread and cheese.

"Oh, this is good, ma'am!" he said. "Very good."

 14

"Have you come far?" she asked him.

"From Paris," he said.

Now this old woman was a little bit simple and a bit on the deaf side too. When he said Paris, she thought he said Paradise.

"There's a coincidence," she said, "that's where they say my first husband went when he died. I wonder if you know him?"

The traveling man cottoned on fast. "Know him?" he said. "Why, he's my next-door neighbor! He told me to drop in if I happened to be passing."

"How is he, then?" she said.

"He's well enough," said the traveling man, "and he makes the best of things, but to tell you the truth, Paradise isn't all it's cracked up to be. Take clothes, for instance. They don't give you any new clothes. Would you believe this was my best suit that I was buried in?"

The old woman looked him up and down, all rags and tatters.

"It never is!" she cried. "Oh, my poor husband! We buried him in nothing but a winding sheet."

"Like I said," said the traveling man, "he makes the best of things. Says it makes him look a bit like a Roman emperor."

"All the same, I can't have him walking around like that," said the old woman. "Can you hang on a moment? I'll put a few things together for him to wear and you can take them back to him."

"I'd be happy to," said the traveling man.

And while she was doing that he was looking around the kitchen and munching on his bread and cheese.

"The food's not too good either," he said. "I haven't tasted home-baked bread since— well, you know."

"Take the rest of the loaf back with you," she said. "I can soon make some more. And how are you off for cheese?"

"There's no cheese in Paradise."

"Better take that too."

"And no meat either," said the traveling man as he eyed the leg of ham that was hanging over the fireplace. "They're all vegetarians there."

"No meat? Dear, dear!" In went the leg of ham.

"You know what he misses most? It's your homemade apple pie."

"Well, isn't it lucky? I've just made one!"

In went the apple pie, along with a small keg of beer and the old man's pipe and a pouch of tobacco.

"But how am I going to carry all this?" the traveling man said, when she'd pretty well stripped the kitchen bare.

"Why, you can borrow the donkey. Bring him back next time you're passing."

"I will," he said. "I will."

Off went the traveling man, leading the laden donkey.

Back came the second husband, hot and hungry from working out in the fields all day. He went to put the horse away.

What did he find? The donkey—gone!

"Where's the donkey?" he asked her. Then,

"Where's my supper?" said he, for the table was bare. "And where are my Sunday boots?"

Well, it wasn't long before he had the whole story out of her, of the traveling man from Paradise.

"You silly old woman!" he cried, and he was mounting his horse and off down the road lickety-split after his donkey, his boots, and his supper.

He hadn't gone far when he came on a man lying flat on his back by the roadside.

"Are you hurt?" said the farmer.

"I'm fine," said the man. "I just saw the most amazing thing. I saw a man leading a donkey."

"Yes! Where did they go?" said the farmer.

"Up there! Up into the sky, walking up a beam of sunlight as easily as if they were walking along this very road."

"They never did!"

"I'm telling you they did. If you're quick you can still see them. Lie down here. I'll hold your horse for you."

So the farmer gave him his horse to hold and lay down by the roadside, while the traveling

man (for that's who it was, though I dare say you guessed) vaulted into the saddle and was off and away, pausing just long enough to collect the donkey and its load from the wood up the road where he'd hidden it.

"Why did you rush off like that?" the old woman demanded when the farmer limped in at the door. "What have you done with the horse? And why did you call me a silly old woman?" she asked him.

He wasn't going to admit he'd been had for a fool.

"Why, for not waiting till I came home," he said. "So I could lend him the horse. I suppose you'd have let him walk all the way back to Paradise!"

The Fish that Flew and the Hare that Swam

Bulgaria

Georgi's wife, Ana, was pretty and plump, a good housewife and an even better cook. But could she talk! She'd talk to anyone—her mother, her neighbors, the market stall holders, or a total stranger who'd only stopped to ask the way—talk about anything and everything, she would, whatever came into her head.

So when Georgi's plow turned up an old Roman pot full of gold coins one day, he knew it was only a matter of time—and a very short time at that—before the world and his wife and the governor too got to hear of it. And, the governor being no believer in finders-keepers, the two of them would be lucky to end up with the odd coin or two as a reward for finding the gold in the first place.

Then he had an idea.

He went to the market and bought a fine, fat fish and a live hare. He stashed the poor hare in the fishing net he'd set close to the river bank and left the fish high up in a wild cherry tree.

Then home he went to fetch Ana.

"Guess what I've found!" he cried. "Not a word to a soul! It looks like a pot of gold coins. Do you want to come and help me dig it up?"

Of course she did.

So off they went and dug up the gold.

On the way home, he said, "Do you know

 21

what I fancy? I fancy a fine, fat fish for supper to celebrate."

"Fish for supper?" said Ana. "You'll be lucky! You never catch anything in those nets of yours and the market's closed by now."

"Maybe this is our lucky day," said Georgi. "First I found that pot of gold. Now look up there, in the cherry tree. Isn't that a fish?"

"A fine, fat one, by the look of it," said Ana. "Up you go, then, and fetch it down."

So up he went and fetched it down. On they jogged till they came to the river.

"I might as well check my nets as we're passing," said Georgi. "Not that I do ever catch anything. Except that today seems to be my lucky day. Well, well! Look at this! A live hare caught in my fishing net!"

"A fish and a hare!" said Ana. "We shall eat well tonight. And a pot of gold too!"

"Mind you tell no one about that," he said.

"I won't tell a soul," she promised.

So how was it, then, that her mother was soon in on the secret? How come the neighbors were all in the know? All of them

promised not to breathe a word, of course.

So however did the governor get to hear the news? News that brought him galloping hotfoot on his mule, with his clerk jogging behind him on his donkey.

"About that pot of gold you found . . ." said the governor.

"What pot of gold?" said Georgi.

"According to your wife—"

"Oh, my wife!" Georgi shook his head. "She's a sad case, your honor. You won't get a word of sense out of her."

"I'll be the judge of that," said the governor. "Send for Georgi's wife!"

Ana came, fresh from stabling the governor's mule along with the clerk's donkey.

"What pot of gold? Oh, that pot of gold!" said Ana. "You must remember, Georgi! You found it the same day you caught the fish in the cherry tree."

Georgi gave the governor a look as if to say, "You see what I mean? Not a word of sense!"

"He caught a fish in a cherry tree?" said the governor.

"I thought it was a bit odd myself," said Ana. "I mean, fish can't fly, can they? Or climb trees. But when Georgi caught a hare in his fishing net the very same day—"

The governor frowned. He looked at Georgi. Georgi shrugged his shoulders.

"He caught a hare? In his fishing net?" said the governor.

"Alive and kicking, wasn't it, Georgi?" said Ana. "I thought it must be one of those days when odd things happen."

"She has times like this," sighed Georgi. "I don't know if she makes these things up or whether she really believes they happened."

"Oh! Making things up, am I?" scoffed Ana. "And I suppose the clerk's donkey was making things up just now when I heard him tell the governor's mule that the clerk was head over  heels in love and planning to run off with—"

But at this point the clerk was taken by such a fit of coughing that nobody heard the rest.

After Georgi had thumped the clerk hard on the back, "What was that you were saying?" said the governor. "About my clerk?"

Ana didn't answer; she just went rattling on. "'Call that news?' says the governor's mule. 'That's nothing to what my master's been up to. He's only been paying for that lovely new house of his out of the money he skims off from the tax—'"

"Enough!" cried the governor. "A talking mule? Ridiculous! You're right, Georgi. Your wife is clearly off her head."

Off he galloped, on his mule, with the clerk jogging behind him on his donkey.

"Well! What was all that about?" said Georgi.

Ana smiled. "I know I talk too much," she said, "but I do know how to listen too. Every woman in town knows the clerk's sweet on the governor's daughter. Maybe they are planning to run away together. As for the governor creaming off money from the taxes he collects: was there ever a governor who didn't? The wonder is they go on fooling themselves that

nobody knows. Now, about that gold you found—"

"What gold?" said Georgi.

"Don't worry," she said. "I won't tell another soul."

"Humph!" said Georgi. Who was there left to tell? But, wisely, he kept that thought to himself.

The White Wolf
Croatia

Still and silent the old mill stood. Silent, that is, apart from the mice that had made their home there and the birds nesting in the eaves. Quite still, apart from the spiders spinning their webs and the little fish playing in the mill stream, darting in and out of the rotting mill wheel.

Until one day a soldier happened along, looking to settle down now that this particular

war was over, find himself a wife maybe, and maybe start a family. Millering seemed like as good an occupation as any and one thing the army had taught him was that nothing was ever so broke that it couldn't be fixed.

So he set to work, measuring and sawing, hammering and planing.

Muttering, shaking their heads, the villagers watched him.

"Just watch out for the wolf!" they told him.

"What wolf?"

"A great white wolf!"

"She haunts this place!"

"Why do you think the mill's stood empty all these years?"

"A wolf?" scoffed the soldier. "Is that all?" He'd faced a lot worse in battle. "But thanks for tipping me off." He slept with his gun close to hand after that.

Silently through the woods in the moonlight the wolf came stealing down to the mill stream to drink.

She made not a sound—so what was it that woke the soldier? Some sixth sense, maybe,

honed on the battlefield.

There stood the wolf in the moonlight below his window, her coat as white as newfallen snow.

Silently he reached for his gun and carefully aimed it, but just as he was about to pull the trigger the wolf stepped out of her skin and into the water—no longer a wolf but a beautiful young girl with hair as pale as moonlight and skin as white as newfallen snow.

The soldier's heart was filled with love and pity for this beautiful girl trapped in a wolf's skin by some strange enchantment. He watched as she slipped out of the water and into her wolfskin again, bounding silently away into the forest.

"Don't worry!" he whispered. "I'll save you."

Day after day he worked until the mill was finished. Night after night he watched for the white wolf to come again.

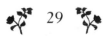

Stealing through the forest she came, slipping out of her skin and into the water.

At once the soldier leaped up from his hiding place, seized the wolfskin, nailed it to the mill wheel, and pulled the lever that set the wheel turning. The wolf-girl howled and held out her arms toward it. *Give me my skin back!* she pleaded with her eyes, for a wolf cannot speak. A wolf cannot weep. She could only crouch at his feet like a dog that's been whipped while he wrapped his cloak around her.

"You're safe now," he told her. "I'll look after you."

She shook her head.

Even so, they were married.

She spoke not a word, not when they were married, nor in all the years after.

A prosperous miller now, he'd joke with his neighbors sometimes, "Don't you wish now and then your wives were as silent as mine?"

But sometimes he'd glance up at the mill wheel turning, turning, with the wolf skin still safely nailed to it, and remember that sad, despairing look she gave him.

In time they had a baby, a little boy, a fine strong lad, already learning the business. And smart too, forever asking questions. "Why doesn't my mother ever speak? Why does she always seem so sad? Is it something to do with that white wolfskin that you've got nailed to the mill wheel?"

"You ask too many questions," said his father.

But people in the village still remembered the great white wolf that used to haunt the mill and had vanished around about the time his mother appeared out of nowhere, so it seemed.

So, little by little, the boy pieced the story together. One day he said to his mother, "I know my father meant to be kind. Instead he did you a great wrong. But I'll put it right!"

One night, soon after that, the miller woke with the uneasy feeling that something was wrong.

The creak and grind of the mill wheel turning, day and night, had become so much part of his life he hardly noticed it. Now all he could hear was the stream rushing by.

He looked out of the window.

Still and silent the mill wheel stood.

Where was the wolfskin? Gone!

Where were his wife and his little son?

In the moonlight below him he saw not one but two white wolves, one smaller than the other.

Then they were gone.

Still and silent the old mill stands. Silent apart from the mice and the birds nesting in the eaves. Still apart from the spiders and the little fish playing.

Somewhere there's an old soldier moving from war to war. "Do you never think of settling down?" they ask him.

"I tried it once," he says sadly. "But it wasn't for me."

Why Dogs Hate Cats

Cyprus

W hy do dogs hate cats?

Some people put it down to envy. Look at it from the dog's point of view. Nobody ever expected a cat to work for its living. Nobody tells a cat to "Sit!" or "Stay!" or "Fetch!" Nobody forces a cat to go for a "Walk!" out in the wind and rain when they've just got themselves comfortable in front of a nice, warm fire. Nobody stops a

cat from climbing on the furniture.

Cats seem to have things all their own way. Whereas dogs . . . !

Others will tell you the rivalry goes back much, much further, to a time before time began.

The animals were holding a conference. The reason for it has long been forgotten, but it must have seemed important at the time. Every species had sent a delegate.

The lion took the chair and the elephant trumpeted the roll-call. Every delegate from the aardvark to the zebra answered "Here!"

All except the camel.

Where was he?

Had anyone seen him?

Maybe. Maybe not. What did he look like?

To be honest, none of them was quite sure. The camel lived in the desert where few of them ever ventured. But his name was on the list. They couldn't start without him. Someone would have to go and fetch him.

The lion looked around. "Would anyone like to volunteer?"

Nobody would.

The fox made a suggestion. "If we all stand around in a circle—and I spin this bottle—" (as to where the fox got hold of a bottle in the time before time began, I can only say, that's foxes for you) "—the  one the bottle points toward when it stops spinning is the one to go and fetch the camel."

He spun the bottle and it ended up pointing toward the dog.

"What's the point in sending me?" said the dog. "I don't even know what a camel looks like."

"No problem," said the fox, "you'll know him the moment you see him by the hump on his back."

Off trotted the dog, searching, searching, till rounding a corner he came quite unexpectedly upon a cat. Which, being as startled as he was at finding the two of them nose to nose, immediately arched its back and fluffed out its fur to twice its size.

Of course what the dog should have said then was, "Are you a camel?" and the cat would have said, "No, of course not." And of course the dog had seen cats before, but never one that looked quite like this. But he was in a hurry. And he'd been on the lookout for a creature with a hump. This one seemed to fit the bill.

"You're late," he said.

"Late for what?" spat the cat.

"Never mind. I haven't got time to explain. Everyone's waiting for us. Come on. This way."

The cat, being curious as cats often are, followed the dog. Being cautious too, it kept its back arched and its fur well fluffed up till they came to the meeting place.

"Here we are!" cried the dog. "Here he is. Here's the camel."

In strolled the cat, keen on looking his best for this unexpected audience, his back no longer arched, his fur sleek as sealskin.

How they all laughed!

They roared. They fell about and clapped one another on the back, tears rolling down their faces. "You thought that was a camel? Are you so stupid you can't tell the difference between a cat and a camel?"

From that day to this, cats have never let dogs forget it. When a cat sees a dog it first of all gives him a look as if to say, "Remember?" Then it arches its back and fluffs out its fur and it's off up a tree, leaving the dog helplessly barking.

But one day he'll get his revenge. One day.

The Mandrake Child
Czech Republic

From the day she was married, Eva dreamed of filling her house with children. Babies to cuddle and toddlers to play with. Sons to be proud of and daughters to keep her company until their turn came to be married. In time there'd be grandchildren.

But time went on, years passed and the children never came.

"Look on the bright side," said her husband. "Children cost money."

And then he died and Eva was left all alone in the world with nothing but a chest full of the money he'd saved to keep her company in her old age. She'd have given it all for one little grandchild to love.

"What do you expect me to do?" the wise woman said. "I can't conjure one for you out of thin air. On the other hand," she added, when she saw the amount of money Eva was offering, "I do have something that might do instead."

She scrabbled around at the bottom of a deep, dark, dusty cupboard and came out clutching—

"What's that?" asked Eva.

"A mandrake root. It looks very like a child, wouldn't you say? Two arms—two legs—one head."

Oh, but so dry and shriveled! More like a changeling than a human child.

"I'll take him!" said Eva.

"Feed it three drops of blood a day—no more!" the wise woman said as Eva wrapped the mandrake root in her shawl.

"Three drops and no more, remember!" the wise woman called after her. "Not that she'll take any notice," she murmured to herself, shaking her head as she hobbled back indoors. "They never do."

As soon as she got home Eva laid the mandrake child in the cradle she'd kept ready all these years.

She pricked her finger with a needle and let three drops of blood fall onto the place where she reckoned its little mouth should be.

Next morning, bright and early, she pricked her finger again. And as the three bright drops of blood fell she saw a tiny mouth open to swallow them up.

Come evening, there lay the poor little thing with its tiny mouth open wide. Surely it could do no harm to feed it again. So she fed it three drops more.

Next morning she fed it again.

Its little mouth opened to lap up the blood and its beady little eyes opened wide.

All day long those eyes watched her. When evening came and she'd fed it again and was about to sit down to her own meal, "Feed me!" it whispered.

What harm could it do to feed it a drop of the soup she'd made for herself? But with each mouthful, "Feed me!" it said, its voice growing stronger—till the soup was all gone. "Feed me!" it still demanded. So she fed it the bread and the cheese she'd been keeping for after and went to bed hungry. But it wasn't so much the hunger that kept her awake all night long as the sound of that mandrake child roaring, "Feed me!"

Morning came and he was out of his cradle and yelling for his breakfast. She fed him all the eggs from the larder and the ham that hung over the fire. With every mouthful he ate, he grew bigger and hungrier.

"Feed me!" he roared.

Poor Eva! She fed him the bread left over from last night, two strings of onions, and a

sack of potatoes. Some carrots and turnips. A sackful of dried beans. The wrinkled remains of last year's apples. She fetched out her store of pickles and jams and as fast as she could scoop them out of the jars he gobbled those up too. She fed him until the larder was bare.

"Feed me!"

"I'm sorry, my darling. There's nothing left."

So he ate her too.

Then out of the door he went and that wasn't easy, the size he'd grown. Off down the road. A dog barked at him so he ate it, along with several of the neighborhood cats; he ate all next door's hens and the rooster as well. A pig and six piglets. A girl milking a goat, complete with the pail, and a shepherd along with his sheep.

And he still went on growing. By the time he came to the wise woman's house he was simply enormous.

"Feed me!" he roared.

"Feed you?" said the wise woman. "I reckon you've already been fed far more than is good for you." Then she took an ax and swung it

 42

and split the mandrake child wide open.

The mandrake child gave a great cry. Slowly, slowly it fell, stone dead.

Then out of the great gaping hole in its stomach came the shepherd and all his sheep, the girl and the goat, the sow and her piglets, the rooster, the chickens, the cats, and the dog. And—first in, last out—poor Eva.

"He kept saying 'Feed me,'" said Eva. "So I did."

"And you think children are the best ones to judge what's good for them?" the wise woman scoffed.

Eva shook her head.

She crept off home, while the wise woman took a firmer grip on her ax and swung it again, and again, and again. *Look on the bright side,* she thought. There should be enough wood here to keep her warm all winter long.

Peter Bull
Denmark

There was a farmer and his wife who had no children. So when the old cow died, leaving a calf with no mother to care for him, they took him in.

They called him Peter.

He was like a son to them. They never could bring themselves to turn him out into the yard with the other animals. He ate when they ate and slept in his own bed on the floor by the

 44

kitchen fire. After a while they started thinking it was about time he was sent to school.

The schoolmaster wasn't a bad man, but he was a poor one. He took the money the farmer offered for Peter's board and lodging and promised to do his best.

Whenever the farmer asked him how Peter was getting on:

"Oh, he's enjoying his studies," the schoolmaster said. "He finds it all most a-moo-sing. He's quite the best behaved pupil I ever had."

Indeed he was; Peter Bull did nothing but stand in a field all day, eating grass.

"When is he coming home to see us?" said the farmer.

"Soon," said the schoolmaster.

"What's he studying now?"

"Geo-moo-try!" The schoolmaster found it hard to keep a straight face.

The next time the farmer asked, the answer was Astronomy.

"Astronomy! Well, well!"

"We go out every night," said the

schoolmaster, chuckling to himself, "and look at the moo-n!"

A month later the answer was, "Moo-sic!"

But the joke was wearing thin. He'd spent the farmer's money, still had Peter Bull to keep, and how could he send him back with no more to say for himself than, "Moo?"

"Music, eh?" said the farmer. "Do you think he could learn to play an instrument? I'd pay extra, of course."

And here was another bag of money being waved under the poor schoolmaster's nose.

"I'm no musician," he said. "We'd have to send him to the city to study."

"We only want the best for our Peter," said the farmer.

So the schoolmaster took the money. Then he took Peter Bull to the city and sold him in the market.

The farmer and his wife waited for news of their adopted son. They waited and waited, but no word came. Not a single letter.

"He's forgotten us," sighed the old man.

The old woman shed a tear.

Then one day they read in the paper that a famous pianist was coming to town. And his name was Peter Bull!

"It must be our Peter!" cried the old man. "I'm going into town to see him."

"Not before I've baked him a cake, you're not," said the little old woman.

The pianist, Peter Bull, was naturally surprised when they told him his old father was there to see him with a cake his mother had baked for him. "But I'm an orphan," he said. "I haven't got a father or a mother."

"We know," said the old man. "Your father died before you were born and your mother, too, soon afterwards. But you were like a son to us. Don't say you've forgotten us, Peter. I know how it is. You've been that busy studying, you just haven't had time to write."

What could the poor pianist say? Especially after he'd tasted that cake!

And when they drove out to the farm, there was the old woman, holding out her arms, weeping tears of joy. "Peter, Peter! You haven't changed. I'd know you anywhere by those

strong shoulders and that little snub nose and that tuft of curly hair that hangs over your forehead."

What could he say? He'd always dreamed of being one of a family. So now he'd got his wish. And he was happy. The farmer and his wife were happy. And so too was the real Peter Bull, living in a field on the other side of the city with a herd of cows for company and all the grass he could eat.

The only loser was the schoolmaster who'd soon spent all the money he'd conned out of the farmer and ended up as poor as before.

The Three Sneezes
Estonia

How long will I live? How much longer have I got? Wouldn't we all like to know? Maybe. On the other hand, maybe not.

As the years went by, the old man could think of nothing else. It was no good the doctor telling him he was as fit as a fiddle— "Yes, but for how much longer?" the old man asked. "How will I know when my time's up?"

 49

The doctor sighed. "When you sneeze three times on the same day," he said, "that's when you'll need to start worrying."

"You mean that'll be the sign that I'm done for?"

"I mean there'll be no need for you to call on me again."

"So all I have to do is not sneeze? Thank you, doctor. Thank you!"

He was careful to keep from sneezing after that, steering clear of anyone with a sniffle or a bit of a cold.

But then came the first fine day of spring. His wife set about the spring cleaning–dusting and sweeping and beating the carpets slung over the washing line. Dust everywhere!

"Stop! Stop!" he cried, as soon as he realized the danger, but by then it was too late.

His nose itched. And twitched. Then he sneezed. "A-choo!"

"That's once," he said. "Twice more and I'm done for."

"I can't help that," said his wife. "I've got to get these carpets clean now I've started. Up

 50

you get, lazybones, and make yourself useful. I've no time for shopping today, so there'll be no bread come suppertime if you don't get yourself down to the mill and fetch me back a sackful of flour."

Off he went to the mill, lickety-split, glad to get out of the house, away from all that dust. But what did he find when he stepped into the mill? Flour flying everywhere! This was no place for a man in mortal fear of sneezing.

He took to his heels, but it was too late.

His nose itched. And twitched. Then he sneezed. "A-choo!"

"That's twice," he said to himself. "Once more and I'm done for."

There's nothing like a brush with death to make a man enjoy life even more. To lift up his face and feel the sunlight. To listen to the birds singing and watch them flying overhead through the blue, blue sky. To smell the flowers—oops!—that was a mistake! Flowers may contain pollen.  Pollen's like dust. It can make your nose

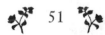

itch and twitch, till you've just got to sneeze.

"A-choo!"

Well, that's it, he thought. *The third sneeze in one day. I'm dead for sure.*

So he lay down, crossed his hands on his chest, and closed his eyes

Time went by and time went by. The cleaning was done and dinner was simmering nicely on the stove, but—no bread!

"Where's he got to?" his wife wondered. "Where's that old lazybones got to? He should have been back long ago with that sack of flour."

So off she went looking. She asked all the neighbors. They hadn't seen him but they offered to help her search. There was quite a crowd tagging along when they finally found him stretched out on the path. Dead as any dead man they'd ever seen, eyes closed and his hands neatly crossed on his chest.

"He did look a bit poorly," the miller admitted when they came to borrow his ladder to use as a stretcher. "Dead now, is he? Ah, well, there you go."

It was a bumpy ride the poor man had of it, coming back down from the mill in the dark, the men carrying the ladder stumbling over the ruts and stones, tossing him this way and that and now—what were they thinking of? Turning left at the crossroads!

"Right! Right!" he shouted. "You should have turned right back there!"

They stopped.

They looked at one another.

They dropped the ladder and they ran. Every last man and woman.

All but his wife, who stood over him, hands on hips. "Get up! Get up, you lazybones," she said. "I never would have believed you would have gone to so much trouble to save yourself from fetching me home a sackful of flour!"

The Fox and the Bear
Finland

It was a cold, cold winter. Snow everywhere. Not a bite to eat for Reynard the Fox or Bruin the Bear.

"Oh, well," sighed Bruin. "We'll just have to wait till spring comes." He curled himself up inside his den and settled down to wait.

Wait till spring for his next meal? Not Reynard. He went on searching, far and wide, high and low.

Not one bite to eat did he find.

Tired out, he lay down by the side of the road.

Along came a man with a wagonload of fish.

Reynard was too tired to run away. Instead he just played dead.

Waste not, want not, thought the man when he saw the fox lying there. *I can sell that fox's skin when I get to the market.*

He tossed Reynard up on top of the load of fish and went jogging along on his way.

Oh, the smell of that fish! Reynard began to feel better already.

Oh, the taste of it on his tongue! Reynard began to eat.

He ate until he was fit to burst. Then he gathered up all the fish he could carry and leaped down into the road, while the wagon went jogging merrily on and out of sight.

Deep in the forest Bruin lay half-awake, half-asleep, waiting for spring, when a strong smell of fish came drifting by.

Bruin was fond of fish.

 55

So up he got, rubbed the sleep from his eyes and followed the smell, till he came to the place where Reynard sat licking his chops.

"Sorry," said Reynard. "I ate the lot. But if you like, I'll show you how you can catch some more."

He led Bruin down to the river to a hole in the ice where the village women had been fetching water.

"All you have to do," said Reynard, "is dip your tail in the water and wait for the fish to bite." (For the bear had a tail in those far-off days, a fine bushy one with a smart white tip.)

"Is that what you did?" said Bruin, hesitating.

"Nothing ventured, nothing gained," said Reynard.

"That's true," said Bruin. "That's very true."

Oh, and he was so—so!—hungry.

So he did as Reynard said. He dipped his tail in the water and sat waiting for the fish to bite.

There Reynard left him.

There Bruin sat.

All night he sat, shivering, waiting for the fish to bite.

Morning came, and still no fish—only the sound of a hunting horn. Followed by the huntsmen and their dogs.

Up jumped Bruin—that's to say, he tried. The hole had frozen over during the night and his tail was stuck fast in the ice. He pulled and he wriggled, with the dogs snapping at his heels and arrows whizzing past his ears, until—until—until his frozen tail snapped right off!

Bruin made for the forest, running and tumbling till the huntsmen and their dogs were left far behind.

At last he stopped and felt for the place where his tail had been.

"Never mind," said Bruin. "It was only one

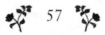

more bit of me to look after. I'm better off
without it."

He set off back to his warm den where he
could sleep till spring came again.

That's why you'll hardly ever see a bear in
the wintertime. And you'll never, ever see one
with a tail.

The Pope's Mule
France

Paciencia was a mule. But not just any mule. Paciencia was the Pope's mule.

She ate the scraps from the Pope's own table. She drank spring water sweetened with honey. At night she lay on a bed of soft hay. When she carried the Pope on her back through the streets of Avignon she was dressed in silk and cloth of gold.

The people cheered. "Oh, Paciencia! How beautiful she is!"

 59

Jacquot Jacou breezed into town, a young man with his way in the world to make.

"You look a likely lad," said the Pope. "Would you like to look after my mule?"

"I'd be honored," said Jacou, bowing low.

Secretly he hated the job.

Poor Paciencia! No more sweet water. No more titbits from the Pope's own table. She ate her bed of soft hay and had  to lie on the cold, hard ground. Under her silk and cloth of gold her coat grew ragged and dirty.

Paciencia didn't complain. How could she? She was just a mule.

At night Jacou and his friends would take her out and ride on her back, two or three at a time. They teased her and beat her, tied things to her tail, and danced her round and round till she was dizzy.

One terrible night they dragged her through the sleeping town and up a narrow flight of steps.

Onward and upward they led her, to the very top of the bell tower.

And there they left her. Poor Paciencia!

The sun came up and the bells began to ring.

"Help me!" she brayed. "Help me, please!"

People came tumbling out of their houses to see the funniest sight in donkey's years. A mule on top of the bell tower, singing along with the bells!

Funnier still was the sight of her coming down again. They had to build a crane to lift her down, with a cradle slung under her tummy.

Where was Jacou? Over the hills and far away, off to seek his fortune at the emperor's court.

Paciencia slept again on a bed of sweet hay. She ate the scraps from the Pope's table and drank water sweetened with honey. But when she walked through the town of Avignon with the Pope on her back, she knew why the people laughed and smiled.

"Oh, Paciencia! Remember the day?"

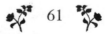

"That day she got stuck on the bell tower. The fun we had, getting her down!"

"The funniest thing you saw in your life!"

Poor Paciencia. Five long years passed and then—Jacquot Jacou came back to Avignon.

No mule-keeper now, he was the Emperor's messenger. The Pope himself came out to meet him, riding on his faithful mule.

"Oh, Paciencia!" cried Jacou. "Remember me? The fun we had together?"

Paciencia remembered but she stood quietly, patiently, until she had Jacou just where she wanted. Then she kicked him. The kick of a mule is a terrible thing and Paciencia was not just any mule. She'd been saving that kick for five long years.

That kick sent Jacou tumbling down the palace steps and through the gate, along the street, and out of the town. If he hasn't stopped yet he's tumbling still.

At last Paciencia could walk through the streets of Avignon again with her head held high. She knew why the people smiled and laughed as she passed.

"Oh, Paciencia! Remember the day?"

"That day she gave that rascal Jacou such a kick!"

"Kicked him right out of town, she did!"

"Paciencia the proud!"

"Paciencia the strong!"

"Paciencia the beautiful!"

Paciencia, the Pope's own, very special mule.

Mannikin
Spannalong
Germany

There was a girl who set out one day to make her own way in the world by the work of her own two hands.

She walked and she walked and when night came there was only one house she could see where she might seek shelter for the night. She knocked and the door swung open.

Inside, sitting cross-legged on the table, was the strangest creature she'd ever seen.

It was no taller than a year-old baby, but it had the face of an old, old man, with bony shoulders and elbows and knees sticking out from under a long, long beard that wound around and around him with enough left over to trail off the edge of the table and onto the floor.

He said:

"I am the Mannikin Spannalong.
I have a beard that's ten ells long.
Girl! Come in and make my supper."

So in she came and made him his supper and set it on the table in front of him so he could eat.

When she'd cleared away and washed the dishes, he said:

"I am the Mannikin Spannalong.
I have a beard that's ten ells long.
Girl! Put me to bed."

So she turned down the covers, undressed him and helped him into his little bed, and arranged his long beard over him to make a quilt.

Then she lay down and slept on the floor beside the fire.

In the morning when he woke up, he said:

> "I am the Mannikin Spannalong.
> I have a beard that's ten ells long.
> Girl! Help me to dress."

So she helped him back into his little shirt and little trousers, his waistcoat and jacket, and his little shoes.

When it was done he said:

> "I am the Mannikin Spannalong.
> I have a beard that's ten ells long.
> Girl! Comb my beard."

So she found a comb and she combed his beard—all ten ells of it!

And the strangest thing began to happen.

The more she combed it, the shorter it grew. As fast as the beard grew shorter the mannikin grew taller. And younger. Until there, standing in front of her, was a very fine young man while the beard lay in piles around her on the floor.

And I suppose you think he asked her to marry him.

Well, he didn't.

Nor did she want him to. She wanted to make her own way in the world by the work of her own two hands.

He thanked her kindly for freeing him from the spell he'd been under and said she could keep the cottage and everything in it, right down to the pile of hair from his beard.

Then off he went to find his own people and that was the last she saw of him.

She looked at the pile of hair—so soft! So fine!

Waste not, want not, she thought.

Out of nothing but a stick and a potato she fashioned herself a spindle and she spun that hair into the softest, finest yarn that ever was seen.

She got a good price for it in the market.

Then she went back to the cottage to spin some more. Soon she'd saved up enough money to buy herself a spinning wheel. After that there was no stopping her.

No matter how fast she spun, the pile of hair never grew less. The more she spun the more there was to do.

The more she spun, the more money she made.

So she made her own way in the world by the work of her own two hands, and if she hasn't died yet, why then, she's spinning still.

The House of the Cats

Greece

There was an old woman who got by with a spot of cleaning here and a bit of sewing there. An hour or two babysitting in some other place.

Still there were times when she went to bed hungry. Then came the night, a cold night too, when she came home from gathering wood for the fire only to find the fire had gone out. And she'd not so much as a match left to light it with.

 69

She looked out of the window to see which of her neighbors were still up and about, but it was late. There were only two other houses where a light still shone. One was the house opposite where a woman lived who was so mean she wouldn't give you so much as a smile without tallying up what you owed her for it. The other was the house at the end. She didn't know the people there, but she'd seen several cats going in and out. *They must be kind*, she thought, *if they're fond of cats.*

So plucking up her courage along with her shawl, off she went to the house at the end and knocked.

The door opened.

There stood a great black cat.

Thinking the owner was maybe hidden by the door, the old woman raised her voice a little. "I'm sorry to trouble you," she said, "at this late hour, but

do you think you could spare me a light for my fire?"

No answer came, but the cat stood back as if inviting her to come in.

So in she went—still no sign of the owner—and followed the big black cat down the hall and into a room that was furnished with couches and cushions. A fire was blazing on the hearth and in front of it stood a long, low table laden with good things to eat.

And there were cats everywhere! Black, white, and ginger. Tabby and tortoiseshell. Stately old tomcats and sprightly kittens.

Still looking around for some sign of people, the old woman bobbed a little curtsey and said, "Good evening to you, one and all."

"Sit down," said the big black cat. "And help yourself."

Well, if she hadn't been so cold and hungry, she would have taken to her heels that instant. As it was—"Bless you!" she said. "Bless you all!" Then she sat down and ate her fill. She was gazing sorrowfully at all the food left over when the big black cat said, "If you'll fetch a

bag, we'll give you something to tide you over the next few days or so."

She was ashamed to admit to being so poor she'd not so much as an old sack.

Off she went with no choice now but to knock at the window of the house opposite until it was flung open.

"What is it?" snapped the neighbor.

"Do you have such a thing as a bag I could borrow, just for half an hour? An old flour sack, even? I'll bring it straight back, I promise."

"Make sure you do!"

Out flew the sack and the window slammed shut before she could murmur a thank you.

Back she went to the House of the Cats and gave the sack to the big black cat.

Ten minutes later when he gave it back, the sack was full to bursting.

Off she went, home again, feeling the sack, trying to guess what was in it, like a child on Christmas morning.

What was her surprise when she emptied it out onto the kitchen table, expecting to find

the leftovers from dinner. It was a heap of gold coins! Enough to keep her in comfort for the rest of her days.

Remembering she'd promised to take the sack straight back to her neighbor, she slipped a gold coin into the corner by way of a thank you.

Next thing she knew the neighbor was hammering on her door. "Where did you get this?" she demanded, holding out the gold piece.

"Why, from the house at the end of the road. The cats said if I brought them a sack—and since you were kind enough to lend it—"

The neighbor didn't let her finish. Off she went, with the sack in her hand, straight to the House of the Cats. When the big black cat opened the door she kicked it out of the way and stormed through the house. "I smell thievery!" she shrieked. "I smell witchcraft! I'm going straight to

the police, this very minute, if you don't fill this sack up for me, just as you did for my neighbor."

Out of the shadows stole the big black cat. Took the sack from her without a word. Came back with it bulging a few minutes later.

Off went the neighbor with her ill-gotten gains.

She was careful to lock the door and draw the curtains, so no one could see her good fortune, before she emptied the sack onto the kitchen table.

Out poured a swarm of wasps. After them, red ants and scorpions. Snakes, hornets, and mosquitoes. They stung and bit her, crawled inside her clothes, and caught in her hair.

She screamed and screamed. She ran for the door and struggled with the lock. Outside, she ran and ran till she came to the river and plunged into the cooling water. And the river carried her away.

Next morning the House of the Cats stood dark and empty. But on her doorstep the old woman found a kitten. She took it in and it

soon grew into a big black cat. She used to chat to it a lot. No one ever heard it answer, but that's not to say it never did.

The Magical Fiddle

Hungary

There was a young man who owned nothing but the clothes on his back and a fiddle. But such a fiddle! Such tunes it played! Tunes to set the whole world dancing or dreaming. Tunes that would make you laugh or weep.

And so he made his way through life, playing his fiddle at weddings and christenings, at fairs and feast days, at cafes and inns, and in market squares.

And what if he did sometimes go hungry? What if he did sometimes spend the night under the stars with only a stone for his pillow? He was free and he had his music.

There was just the odd time when he thought how it would be if he were to settle down in his own place with its own bit of land and a dog and a goat, a few hens, and maybe even a pig.

So lost was he in this dream as he trudged the road one rainy night between the last fair and the next wedding that when he turned a corner and came upon a little house so exactly like the place he'd been thinking of, he thought at first he might have conjured it with his music.

But the door seemed solid enough when he knocked on it. And the little old man who opened it was like nothing out of his dreams or his nightmares.

"Come in!" said the old man. "I've been expecting you. Come in and make yourself at home."

Come in he did. He ate and drank his fill,

warmed himself by the hearth, and slept that night on a soft feather bed.

"You know," he said to the little old man next morning, "I've dreamed sometimes of owning a place just like this."

"I know," said the little old man. "And it's yours. All I ask in exchange is your fiddle."

"My fiddle? I'm sorry, but I'm booked to play at a wedding tomorrow."

"I can play at the wedding for you. You won't get an offer like this again. Come on! Shake hands and a bargain."

So the young man handed over his fiddle. Off went the little old man, over the hills and far away, while the fiddler did his best to settle down. After all, wasn't this the home he'd always dreamed of?

He made friends with the dog. He milked the goat. He collected the eggs. He fed the pig and he dug the vegetable patch.

Oh, but he missed the freedom of the open road, of never knowing what each new day would bring.

Mostly he missed the sound of the fiddle.

He tried humming and whistling but it wasn't the same.

More and more he thought about the little old man. The more he thought, the more it seemed he'd seen that face, not once, but many times before. As a guest at a wedding. A peddler at a fair. A waiter in a restaurant. A beggar on the street corner. As if the old man had been watching him for a long, long time.

"I've been expecting you," the little old man had said.

And wasn't this place too exactly like the place of his dreams to be real?

Each morning he woke half expecting the house to have vanished away in the night.

On the other hand, they'd made a bargain: this place in exchange for his fiddle. As long as the little old man had the fiddle, then this was his home and he was stuck with it.

Then one day there came a hammering on the door. There stood the little old man with the fiddle in his hand and his face screwed up like an old wizened apple. "You cheated me!" he screamed.

"Cheated you how? You have my fiddle."

"I have the fiddle, but where's the magic? I've followed you from fair to fair. I've heard you play. This fiddle should have given me power over everyone who heard it, to make them laugh or weep, to dance or dream." He sank down on the step and began to sob. "They set the dogs on me at the wedding. At the midsummer fair they threw things. I've been kicked out of cafes and locked up in 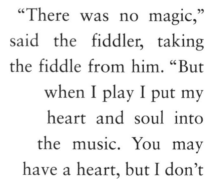 jail only for playing in the street. What happened to the magic? What did you do with it?"

"There was no magic," said the fiddler, taking the fiddle from him. "But when I play I put my heart and soul into the music. You may have a heart, but I don't think those of your kind have a soul."

"My kind! What is my kind?" spat the little old man.

"Not human kind, I'm thinking. I think

you're one of those we call the Fair Folk. As to whether you're a gnome or a goblin or a gremlin, I'm not qualified to judge. But one thing I do know: you may be able to spin the home of my dreams for me out of thin air, but a fiddler you can never be."

Then the fiddler set the fiddle under his chin and began to play such a merry tune that the old man forgot his tears and began to dance.

The fiddler glanced back once as he walked away.

The house of his dreams had faded away but the old man was still there dancing.

He glanced back a second time and the old man was gone.

Ahead of him lay the open road. Maybe he'd sleep under the stars tonight with a cold, hard stone for his pillow. Who knew where his next meal would come from or what tomorrow would bring?

But what of that? He was a free man and he had his music.

Munachar and Manachar

Ireland

Munachar and Manachar went picking blackberries one day. Between them they picked a tidy few.

Then Manachar got tired of picking and started eating. As fast as Munachar was putting them in the basket, Manachar was popping them into his mouth.

"Stop that!" said Munachar.

"I won't," said Manachar.

"I'll make you, then," said Munachar.

"You and whose army?" said Manachar.

"Me and the biggest, hardest stick I can find to beat you with!"

Off went Munachar, taking the basket of blackberries with him so Manachar couldn't steal any more while he was gone.

Munachar couldn't find a stick anywhere.

So he walked on with his basket of blackberries until he came to a tree.

"Tree, if you please," said Munachar, "will you let me have a stick so I can beat Manachar and stop him from eating all the blackberries?"

"I will," said the tree, "if you can find an ax to cut it with."

So Munachar walked on with his basket of blackberries till he found an ax propped up against a tree stump where the woodman had left it while he went off for his dinner.

"If you please, ax," said Munachar, "will you help me cut a stick from that tree over there, so I can beat Manachar with it and stop him from eating all the blackberries?"

"I will," said the ax, "if you can find a stone to sharpen me on."

So Munachar walked on, still carrying his basket of blackberries, till he found a likely-looking stone.

"Stone," said Munachar, "will you please help me sharpen that ax over there so I can cut a stick from the tree and beat Manachar to stop him from eating all the blackberries?"

"I will," said the stone, "if you will find some water to wet me with."

So on went Munachar, still carrying the blackberries, till he came to a pool of water.

"Please, water," said Munachar, "will you help me wet the stone so I can sharpen the ax to cut a stick from the tree, so I can beat Manachar with it and stop him from eating all the blackberries?"

"I will," said the water, "if you will find a bucket to fetch me in."

So Munachar walked on. Were his blackberries still safe? Yes, they were.

He came to a cottage where a little old woman was working in the kitchen.

"Please," said Munachar, "will you lend me a bucket to fetch some water to wet the stone to sharpen the ax to cut a branch so I can beat Manachar and stop him from eating all the blackberries?"

"I will," said the old woman, "if you will fetch me some flour from the miller so I can make an apple pie."

So Munachar walked on with his blackberries until he came to the mill.

"Please," said Munachar to the miller, "will you give me some flour for the old lady to make an apple pie so she'll lend me a bucket to fetch some water to wet the stone to sharpen the ax to cut a stick from the tree so I can beat Manachar with it and stop him from eating all the blackberries?"

"I will," said the miller. "What will you pay me for it?"

Munachar had nothing to pay him with but the blackberries.

So he gave him those.

He took the flour to the old lady, so she could make her apple pie.

He took the bucket to fetch the water.

He used the water to wet the stone.

He took the stone to sharpen the ax.

He took the ax and cut himself a fine, big stick from the tree.

He took the stick so he could beat Manachar with it and stop him from eating all the blackberries.

But Manachar had long ago gone home.

As for the blackberries, the miller had them for his tea. Very good they were too.

A Very Expensive Omelette

Italy

There was a young man who was as poor as poor could be and it bothered him not one bit till he fell in love with a farmer's daughter, the prettiest girl in the whole wide world.

So off he went to seek his fortune and she promised to wait for him till he came back.

He'd signed on to work as a deckhand on a

boat that was leaving next day and he didn't mind sleeping rough that last night on shore, but he was mortally hungry. So he went to an inn by the harbor and he said to the landlady, "I've no money on me at present, but if you'd be kind enough to cook something for me I'll pay you for it when I come back."

"How do I know you will come back?" she said.

"Because I'm engaged to be married to the prettiest girl in the whole wide world!"

"Fair enough," said the landlady. "I can cook you an omelette. What would you like in it? Cheese? Bacon? Or mushrooms?"

"Bacon, I think," he said.

"Bacon it shall be."

So she cooked him his omelette, and very good it tasted—to a man near starving. (She was actually a terrible cook.)

Off he went next morning to make his fortune.

Back he came after five long years, a rich man now, ready to claim his bride.

She was ready and willing to marry him.

But first he had to settle his debt.

What a shock he had when he saw the bill. "Three eggs," said the landlady, "went into that omelette you ate. But if those eggs had hatched, they'd have grown into chickens. Those chickens would have laid eggs in their turn, which would have hatched into still more chickens, who'd have laid more eggs, and so on and so forth. I could have made a tidy profit from selling those chickens and eggs, if you hadn't eaten those eggs in the first place. That's without the pig that was killed to make the bacon that went into it. That pig, if she'd lived, would have had piglets. Those piglets would have had more piglets and—"

"Stop! Stop!" cried the young man. "I can't pay this." If he did, he'd be as poor as before.

"Can't or won't?" said the landlady. "You'll pay it in full or I'll have the law on you."

And she did, but not before he'd had a chance to pour out his troubles to the farmer's daughter who, in spite of being five years older, was still the prettiest girl in the whole wide world.

She'd waited five years for him. She wasn't about to let him slip through her fingers now.

"Don't worry," she said as they led him away to jail. "I'll stand by you, no matter what."

So, come the day of the trial, where was she?

Such a crowd there was in the courtroom that day, come to see the local boy made good about to be made a beggar again if the landlady had her way. All of them hoping it wouldn't be so; apart from her being a terrible cook, there was a strong suspicion that the landlady was in the habit of watering down her wine.

Even in such a crowd, the young man would have picked out the face of his own true love in a moment if she'd been there.

But she wasn't.

In came the judge, resplendent in his robes, followed by the clerk of the court.

"I'll stand by you," the farmer's daughter had said. So where was she?

The charge was read out, the bill produced.

"All this? For one omelette?" said the judge, bemused.

"Three eggs at compound interest," the clerk pointed out, "over five years."

"I see." The judge nodded wisely, though he'd never been any good at math. "Well, I suppose that's fair enough. And what have you to say, young man, in your defense?"

"I speak for the defense!" cried a voice from the back of the crowd.

"Silence in court!" cried the clerk.

"No, no!" said the judge. "We must hear the defense. Let her through. You're not a lawyer, my dear," he said to the prettiest girl in the world when she curtsied before him.

"No, your honor. But we're engaged to be married. Five long years I've waited for him. I think that gives me the right to speak,

don't you? First let me say, I'm truly sorry I'm late, but I'm a farmer's daughter and I had to finish roasting the wheat ready for planting tomorrow."

"Roasting the wheat?" echoed the judge. "Ready for planting? And you a farmer's daughter! Surely you know that once it's been roasted, that wheat will never grow?"

"As sure as I know," she nodded, "that an egg that's been broken will never hatch into a chick. And a pig that's been killed for bacon will never produce piglets." She smiled.

The judge smiled back. He couldn't help himself, for she really was the prettiest girl in all the world. "And the landlady broke the eggs of her own free will—nobody forced her to do it—and she it was who ordered the pig to be slaughtered and turned into bacon. Is that your defense, my dear?"

"Your honor puts it so much better than I ever could."

"Case dismissed!" cried the judge and everyone cheered. "You're a lucky man," he said.

"I know," said the young man, hugging his bride-to-be.

"You don't know how lucky," said the judge. "If I were thirty years younger—but I'm not! As for you, madam—" He turned to the landlady. "Don't go away yet. I've been getting complaints of late about watered-down wine."

Misery

Latvia

At school they'd been the best of friends, as close as two peas in a pod. If you saw one, odds were the other was no more than whistling distance away.

But as they grew older, they grew apart. One of them had the Midas touch. Money just seemed to stick to his fingers. Whatever he invested in turned a profit.

The other grew poorer by the day. If the

sun didn't burn his crops to a frazzle, the rain beat them down into the mud before he could harvest. His cow stopped giving milk almost as soon as he bought it. His hens didn't lay and there wasn't enough meat on them to make one good meal for his growing family.

None of them could pinpoint the moment when Hope deserted them and Misery crept in at the door; so silently he came, like a shadow passing overhead on a clear, sunny day. The sound of him was no more than a sigh. But there he was and there he stayed, crouched in the chimney corner, growing stronger with each new disaster.

The chimney smoked. The roof leaked. The wind blew in and out through the broken window panes. The pig sickened and died.

The poor man went at last, cap in hand, to his old school friend for a small loan, just enough to tide them over: "I never mix business with friendship," the rich man said. "But I tell you what. It's my birthday tomorrow. Come to the party! Bring the wife."

They'd never felt less like partying, but, "We might manage to smuggle out a few leftovers for the children," said his wife. So off they went.

Of course Misery came too, huddling beside them where they sat in a corner, ignored by everyone, including the servants carrying around the food and drink.

Misery's not exactly catching, but nobody likes to get too close.

As for the chance of smuggling out a few leftovers for the children—forget it.

"I should send you away," the poor man said to his wife as they trudged home. "You could take the children to your mother's for a bit."

"And leave you here at the mercy of old Misery? Never! He'll think he's won."

"We've got to do something." The poor man shook his head.

He thought about it all the next day while he watched the children playing. They couldn't afford any toys, of course, but they could always come up with some game to play. Today it was follow-the-leader, dodging in

and out among the forest trees, dancing over rocks, and crawling through a hollow log.

That gave him an idea. He called his wife and whispered in her ear.

She smiled.

What's he up to? Misery wondered. *Why is she smiling? She's got no right to smile like that!*

"Can we play too?" the poor man cried. "Can I be leader?"

Of course he could.

Where's he off to? Misery wondered. *Looks like he's having fun. I can't have that!*

So as the new game of follow-the-leader set off, Misery tagged on the end.

A merry dance the poor man led them, in and out of the forest trees, skipping over the rocks, and finally crawling through that old hollow log. Then, as the last and smallest child crawled out, the man rolled a rock into place to stop the hole and hammered in a stout wooden peg to hold it in place.

Misery started shuffling backward. But that way was blocked too, by another rock.

Misery was trapped.

"And there you'll stay!" roared the poor man.

From that moment on his luck began to change. When he'd moved the rock to stop the hole, he'd noticed a bit of old sacking buried underneath. When he went back to look, it turned out to be a bag of gold coins, enough to restock the farm, do up the house, buy himself a horse and cart, and still have a bit left over for a rainy day.

At first he couldn't believe his luck. He went back every day to the hollow log to check that Misery was still trapped inside.

The rich man couldn't believe his eyes when he saw his old friend who'd been begging him for a handout driving into town in a horse and cart much finer than his own, and all the family tricked out in the very best that money could buy.

He watched him and he followed him down to the woods. Saw him check out the old hollow log, making sure the rocks that sealed the ends were still firmly in place.

"So that's where he keeps his money!" he said to himself. "The miser. The liar. He had even me half-believing that sob story about not having enough to tide them through the winter. So how much has he got stashed away? Let's see."

As soon as he rolled away the stone, out leapt Misery, as large as life and twice as nasty as before, and he fastened himself onto the rich man's shoulders.

"Now I've got you!" screamed Misery. "This time I'll never let you go! I'm going to make you pay and pay and pay for shutting me up inside that log!"

"It wasn't me! You've got the wrong man!" But the rich man's protesting did no good. From that day on his good luck changed to bad.

So the wheel of fortune keeps on turning.

The Amber Princess

Lithuania

"Hush, my darling! My precious, my angel," the Storm King crooned to his little daughter, rocking the baby in his arms. "Don't cry, Jurate."

But the rocking was like being tossed on a stormy sea, the sound of his voice was like thunder, and the clouds she was wrapped in were cold and damp. Little Jurate went on crying.

Deep beneath the Baltic Sea, the Storm

King built a palace of amber; shades of red-gold, honey-gold, and green glowing softly in the sunlight filtered down from the world above. As the waves moved back and forth, patterns of light and shadow rippled across the rocky floor. The baby stopped crying, chuckled, and held out her chubby arms trying to catch them.

There in the amber palace deep beneath the Baltic Sea the Storm King left his daughter. The seals cradled her and the whales sang lullabies. The crabs scuttling sideways made her laugh and the little fishes played with her, in and out of the shifting fronds of seaweed.

So she grew, surrounded by creatures who cared for her. So the sadness inside her grew too—a sadness that drove her to swim further and further from the safety of the amber palace, seeking she knew not what.

On the shore of the Baltic Sea there lived a young fisherman, quite alone. On fine days he sailed out and cast his nets and caught just enough to sell in the market to keep body and

101

soul together. Such was his lonely life and such it would be till the day he died. Or so it seemed.

Then one day he hauled up a catch like he'd never seen before. Big as a seal, it was, and thrashing and writhing. He hardly had the strength to haul it aboard before they both collapsed, exhausted. And he saw it wasn't a seal at all.

It was a girl. A girl with red-gold hair and sea-green eyes and skin as pale as fine sand with shadows rippling over it like sunlight through clear water.

"Are you a mermaid?" he asked her.

"A mermaid!" She laughed, and he thought it was the most beautiful sound he had ever heard. "I am Jurate, the Storm King's daughter."

Then she saw the fish he'd caught, lying in the bottom of the boat.

"Are you going to eat all these?" she asked in amazement.

He shook his head. "Some I'll eat. The rest I'll sell."

"Sell? How?"

"In the market."

"Why?"

"Why? So I can buy things."

"What things?"

"Things I need. Like clothes, bread, milk, wood for the fire—"

"Why do you need these things?"

"Doesn't everyone?"

"I don't. Explain to me why you need them."

But before he was even halfway through explaining how things were in the world above, the sun went down and the moon and the stars were coming out.

"I must go," she said. "My people will be worried."

"Will I see you again?"

"Oh, yes."

"How will I know where to find you?"

"Don't worry. I have my spies! I'll find you."

Day after day they met after that. Sometimes she came to him, where he sat on the rocky

shore. Sometimes he sailed out across the water and cast his nets, though he barely caught enough to feed himself before Jurate was there and they fell to talking again.

What did they find to talk about? A thousand things! Things that were everyday and boring to him—houses and shops, horses and carts, farm animals, flowers in spring and fruit in autumn—were suddenly full of wonder. In return, Jurate painted a word-picture for him of the amber palace under the sea. "Come with me and I'll show you."

He shook his head. "I can't even swim, never mind breathe underwater. But come with me and I'll show you my world."

"I'd die in your world," she said. "Too long in the sunlight and I'd wither away."

So, in this place between the worlds, they met day after day and they fell in love.

But Jurate was not the only one who had her spies. One evening as the fisherman turned his boat toward home and Jurate swam back to her amber palace, she found her father, the Storm King, waiting.

"You can't love a mortal!" the Storm King thundered.

Jurate defied him. "I can! I do!"

"I forbid it!" he roared. The doors of the amber palace slammed shut. Jurate was a prisoner.

Far and wide across the sea the Storm King went searching for the fisherman who'd tried to steal away his daughter.

Long before the little boat reached the safety of the shore, dark clouds came tumbling across the sky, turning bright day to darkest night. Lashed by the waves from all directions, the little boat was tossed like a cork. The lightning flashed and the thunder crashed. The waves rose higher and higher. The mast was broken, the sail torn to shreds, and the oars borne away on the waters.

The fisherman clung for his life to the upturned hull.

"Jurate!" he cried as another wave carried him skywards again, the waters drawing so far back from the ocean bed that in his dying moments he caught one glimpse of the

wonderful amber palace before the little boat was smashed to smithereens.

Such was the Storm King's rage that, before it was done, he'd broken the amber palace he'd built for his daughter into a million pieces. The winds and the waves and the little fishes carried the fragments north, south, east, and west, scattering them all along the Baltic seashore, where they can still be found to this day.

As for Jurate, with the amber palace gone she was free again, free to roam the seas forever, searching, weeping, for her lost, drowned love.

Melusina

Luxembourg

Count Siegfried was young and rich and handsome and the ruler of a county which was, admittedly, on the small side but whose people were as prosperous and happy as anywhere in Europe. He could have married any girl he chose.

Instead he'd fallen head over heels in love with a nobody. A chit! A minx! A fortune-

hunter! Where did she come from, this Melusina? That was the question being asked the length and breadth of Luxembourg, by all the mothers with daughters who'd seen the best marriage prospect in the county snatched from under their very noses.

The story was that, while out hunting, Count Siegfried had been lured away from his friends by the sound of a woman singing a song that only he seemed to hear. Till he came to a mountain spring running into a pool where he found Melusina bathing. The count—being a gentleman to his fingertips, God bless him—swiftly offered her his cloak to cover her nakedness. And then he asked her to marry him! Just like that.

Love at first sight? The gossips shook their heads. No good would come of this marriage, they said. Then they sat back and waited for time to prove them right.

Time passed. The couple were happy, but— "Why is it," the gossips wondered aloud, "that the countess is never seen in church on a Sunday?"

Why, said the count, because the countess had her own chapel in the palace, to which she retired at sunset on Saturdays, to spend all day Sunday in prayer and meditation.

Oh! Really? What god did she pray to, though? Maybe she wasn't even a Christian! If even the count wasn't allowed to join her, wasn't it more likely that she was a witch who spent every Sunday brewing spells to keep the poor man bound to her heart and soul?

The count did love his wife heart and soul. He was sure there was no witchcraft in it, but he knew no more than anyone else what his wife did locked away every Sunday.

It wasn't so bad before the children were born; together he and his Melusina would defy the world!

But each time a baby was born the gossips found some fault in it. Weren't this one's ears unnaturally big? That one definitely had eyes of two different colors, which was strange, to say the least. As for the next—whoever heard of a baby born covered all over in hair like an animal? Another had

such a red face—well, you couldn't say that was just a birthmark, could you?

Count Siegfried loved his wife and he loved his children, but at last the whispers and the sly looks and knowing nods drove him to do what he'd sworn to Melusina he never would.

One Saturday night, after she'd locked herself into her private chapel, Count Siegfried crept to the door. He bent down and peeped through the keyhole—and what did he see?

He saw his wife, in her bath, looking just as she'd looked the first time he saw her.

Then he caught his breath. Was it possible he'd not noticed on that day in the forest the long, snake-like tail trailing over the side of the bath?

She wasn't just a witch; she was a monster!

He must have made some sound. A sigh. A sob. An almost-cry, quickly stifled. Somehow she knew he'd seen her.

Some say the floor split open then and

swallowed her up, bath and all. "Straight down to hell where she belongs!" cried the gossips, triumphant.

Some say she dived straight out of the window and into the river below.

And some say she gave an eldritch shriek that turned the hair white of all who heard it and, in an instant, flew out of the window, went three times around the castle and then away.

What they all seemed to agree on was that she was never seen again.

But often during the weeks and months that followed, the nurses who looked after her two youngest children would be woken at night by the sound of a woman singing. Such a sweet, sad song it was, it lulled them to sleep again. When at last they went to check on the children, they found nobody there, only the night wind blowing in through the open window, and the cradles gently rocking.

The Happy Man
Malta

There was once a king who ruled his land both wisely and well. The country was prosperous and the people contented. He had a beautiful wife who loved him and a handsome son.

So what was it that ailed him? The king hardly ate. He couldn't sleep. There were days when he couldn't be bothered to get out of bed. When he did get up, he'd sit, hour after hour, gazing sadly out of the window.

 112

Was he ill?

The doctors examined him from top to toe and shook their heads. He wasn't ill.

Was it affairs of state?

His ministers all agreed the kingdom was in tip-top condition. Things had never been better.

The queen was at her wits' end when one day an old fortune-teller woman came knocking at the palace door. Before the guards could throw her out, "I can tell you what ails the king," she cried, "and I can tell you how to cure him! The king will not recover," she told the queen, "until the day he wears the shirt of a truly happy man."

The queen told the king the good news. "All we have to do is find a truly happy man and ask him to give you his shirt."

The king sighed. "If you say so, my love."

Naturally they started at the top.

"Are you happy?" they asked the chief minister.

"I would be," he said, "if it wasn't for the cares of the kingdom resting on my unworthy shoulders."

"I thought the kingdom was supposed to be doing rather well," said the queen.

"That's no reason not to worry, is it?"

The queen asked the crown prince, "Are you happy?"

"Of course I am, Mother."

"Of course you are. You'll be king someday."

"What I'd really like to be is a sailor and travel the world!"

"So you're not really happy, then?"

"Sorry. No."

Next she asked the court jester, a man who used to keep the king laughing all evening. Was he happy? No, he was not. There was

this girl who loved him dearly, but she didn't want a husband who had people falling over themselves laughing every time he walked into a room.

"Are you happy?" she asked a victorious general as she pinned another medal on his chest.

"How can I be, your majesty, when I think of all those brave fellows who've died fighting in the battles I've won?"

As for the richest man in the kingdom—didn't he spend every moment, every waking hour, worrying that he might lose it all?

The queen meant well, but in the end the king was sick of it. "Leave me alone!" he cried. He saddled his horse and went riding through the kingdom, which was full of people who seemed to be happy, but he knew better.

At last he came to a wild, lonely seashore and saw a figure coming toward him. It was a man wrapped in a tattered cloak against the biting wind. He carried a shrimping net in one hand and a basket of shrimps in the other.

"Would you like some?" said the man. He led the king to a cave on the seashore where a fire was smoldering. He added some sticks of driftwood to the fire, filled a pan with water from a spring of fresh water nearby, and tossed the shrimps into the pan to cook.

"Is this where you live?" said the king, looking around.

"It is," said the man. "Do you like it?"

"It's—different," said the king politely.

"What more does a man need but a roof over his head, a bed of fresh bracken, a supply of fresh water, and wood for the fire?"

"What do you eat?" the king asked. "Apart from shrimps. These are very good, by the way."

"Fish from the sea," said the man. "And sea birds' eggs. There's a fine apple tree on the cliff above. Blackberries in season, wild strawberries, and mushrooms."

"But still, you must sometimes go hungry."

"Why, that makes the next meal all the tastier!"

"How do you fill your days?"

"I forage for food. I watch the birds. I swim in the sea. I lie in the sun."

"It strikes me," the king said, "that you are a truly happy man."

"I suppose I am."

"Give me your shirt!" the king demanded.

"But—"

"But me no buts! I am your king and I want your shirt!"

The man smiled and shook his head. Slowly he unwound his cloak. "You'd be welcome to my shirt," he said, "if I had one."

There he stood, in nothing but a pair of tattered trousers.

The one truly happy man in the kingdom didn't even own a shirt.

Tyl Uilenspiegel, Painter

Netherlands

S o you're a painter now, Tyl," said the landgraaf.

"Painter to the nobility," said Tyl Uilenspiegel, bowing very low. The landgraaf was after all the chief man in those parts and entitled to a show of respect. And a show of respect was all it was, thought the landgraaf, who knew Tyl and his tricks of old.

What's he up to this time? the landgraaf wondered. There was only one way to find out. That was to play along.

"So you'd be willing to paint a few portraits of my courtiers?" he said.

"I'd be honored," said Tyl. "And—just for you, landgraaf—there'll be no charge. Only give me a place to work, a bed to sleep on, and three square meals a day."

"Done," said the landgraaf. "I'll give you a month's trial. But, if at the end of a month I find that you haven't painted the people I send you just the way I see them with these two eyes of mine, I warn you, you'll be spending a lot longer than a month in a very dark, damp place, with nothing but bread and water to eat and the cold, hard floor to sleep on."

"You've got yourself a deal!" Tyl grinned.

First up was a gouty old knight with a belly the size of a beer barrel who turned himself sideways and said proudly, "Look at that stomach. Flat as a board! I've not put an inch on my waist since I was a stripling of twenty. So my tailor tells me." *No doubt*, thought Tyl,

taking up his brushes, *the tailor's tape measure would tell a different story.*

"And if you make me look any different," the old man added, "I'll set the dogs on you!"

Next came a young-ish woman with spots like erupting volcanoes, teeth like tombstones, and hair like straw left out in a hailstorm. "This is a portrait for my beloved," she said. "I haven't met him yet, but my brothers say this is my last chance of finding a husband. If he doesn't agree to marry me when he sees this portrait, they're going to string you up by your heels and horsewhip you."

Thick and fast they came after that, crook-backed, pock-marked, beer-bellied, walnut-wrinkled, each of them uglier and vainer than the last. Each of them convinced they'd carry off first prize in any beauty contest, no problem, if they ever forgot their dignity so far as to take part in so common a thing.

Don't any of them own a mirror? Tyl wondered.

Of course the landgraaf was doing it on purpose, sending him the ugliest and the

 120

vainest among his courtiers. *Let's see you wriggle your way out of this, Tyl Uilenspiegel!* he thought to himself.

Tyl went on merrily painting, eating and drinking his fill three times a day, all at the landgraaf's expense, and slept each night on a soft feather bed, as if he'd not a care in the world. As if the thought never entered his head that come the end of the month he was going to be strung up by his thumbs, flayed, disembowelled, boiled alive, torn limb from limb by wild horses, trampled by elephants, and/or die the death of a thousand cuts, to name but a few and in no particular order, depending on who got to him first, if his sitters weren't delighted with their portraits.

Either that, or he'd be swapping the three meals a day and the soft feather bed for a cold, dark cell and a diet of bread and water for a very long time to come.

So how come Tyl was smiling when the great day came and he invited them in to admire his work?

"First," he said, "a word of warning! I told the landgraaf before I began that I am a painter to the nobility—and only the nobility! Whoever among you is truly of noble blood will see him- or herself painted here as truly as if they were looking into a mirror. But whoever is not of noble ancestry—if they have one drop of common blood—of peasant blood, God forbid!—will see nothing but a blank canvas."

He drew back the curtain and what did they see?

Nothing but a row of blank canvasses.

Of course none of them was going to admit it. They were all too vain, too proud of their noble birth.

There was silence for a moment. Then first one, then another began to admire the skill of the painter—the likeness! It was quite uncanny, they all agreed. "As if I was looking at myself in a mirror!"

None of them would admit they might have—somewhere deep in the dim and distant past—a drop of peasant blood.

"What about you, my lord?" Tyl asked the landgraaf, after the rest had gone. "Are you satisfied?"

The landgraaf smiled. "Which one of us can swear, hand on heart, he doesn't have a drop of peasant blood in his veins? But I said if you didn't paint them just as I see them, Tyl, it would be a cold, damp dungeon for you and a diet of bread of water. All I see is a row of blank canvasses and I'm not ashamed to admit it."

"But isn't that just how you see those stuck-up fools?" said Tyl. "Haven't I shown them up for what they truly are? A row of blank canvasses for you to make of what you will."

The landgraaf paused for a moment, considering. Then he laughed aloud. "You're right, you rascal! But I didn't need you to tell me that."

"All the same," said Tyl, "we made a bargain."

"So we did," said the landgraaf. "And you've had a month's board and lodging at my expense."

"You've had a good laugh, though, haven't you?" said Tyl.

"You'd best take yourself off," said the landgraaf, "while I'm still laughing."

Tyl didn't need telling twice.

"You won't catch me so easily the next time!" the landgraaf called after him.

Tyl grinned to himself. "Don't count on it," he murmured.

The Glass Mountain

Poland

Somewhere, deep in the heart of Poland, there is a mountain made of glass.

On top of the mountain stands a palace built of silver where once a princess, beautiful as the dawn and sad as a rainy Sunday, was kept prisoner by an evil magician.

Many brave knights tried to rescue her. Some of them set off at a gallop, hoping to get up enough speed to take them all the way to the top of the glass mountain before they began sliding down again.

Others went more gingerly, wrapping their horses' hooves in woollen cloth to give them more of a grip. They landed the same as the others, in a tangle of blood and broken bones, while overhead the magician soared triumphant in the shape of a great golden eagle.

It was the horses Jan felt sorry for. Jan was a boy who thought about things.

"Wouldn't you stand a better chance," he said to the latest knight to try his luck, "if you got off the horse and went up on your hands and knees?"

"Look at me, boy. I'm a knight!" the knight called over his shoulder. (He was planning to take a really good run up.) "A knight doesn't crawl on his hands and knees."

"How do you know there's a princess up there anyway?"

"Of course she's there."

"Yes, but I mean—I've been thinking about it—nobody's ever seen her, have they? How

long is she supposed to have been up there, anyway? She might be a hideous old crone by now."

"But she's not."

"How do you know?"

"I just do! Now, out of my way, boy! I'm on a quest!"

He did better than most, Jan had to admit. But the end was always the same.

"I told you you'd be better off without the horse," said Jan.

"Stupid boy!" muttered the knight and strode off to kill the next living thing he saw, out of sheer bad temper.

Which happened to be a mountain lion, which up to then had been quietly minding its own business, taking a snooze and dreaming of rabbits and deer.

Jan stood over the poor old lion's body and thought for a bit, till he had an idea.

He cut off the lion's claws and fastened them to his own hands and feet. And he began to climb the glass mountain, hand over hand, step by step, digging his claws in every time.

When night came on he was higher than any of the knights had ever managed, but still a long way from the top. So he dug in his claws extra hard, then did his best to catch some sleep.

Morning came and the people in the town were waking. It wasn't long before somebody looked up at the glass mountain.

"What's that up there?" he said.

"Where?"

"Up there on the glass mountain!"

"It looks like our Jan," said someone with better eyesight than the rest.

"It never is! What's he doing up there?"

"Trying to rescue the princess, I suppose."

"Do you think he might make it?"

"Not if that eagle has anything to do with it."

Alerted by the to-do in the town below, the eagle was already circling. Suddenly, like a tidy housewife spying a speck of dust, it swooped down.

Jan awoke to find himself flying, his belt hooked in the eagle's talons. Below him he

could see the palace of silver. And a girl standing in the courtyard, looking upward. Not an old crone, definitely a girl, though whether she was beautiful or not, never mind sad as a rainy Sunday, he was already too high to see and being carried higher by the minute.

As the eagle soared still higher Jan wriggled around and stabbed at its belly with his lion's claws. The eagle shrieked in pain and fury, but its beak couldn't reach him while it was on the wing and its talons were useless while they were hooked in his belt.

Again and again he slashed. The bird was circling lower now. Its strength was failing. It couldn't hold him. Suddenly—down fell Jan, down, down, and down again.

The eagle flew off, dripping blood, never to be seen again.

As for Jan, luckily his fall was broken by a tree that just happened to be growing in the courtyard of the silver palace. Down he

fell through its branches and landed at the princess's feet.

"My hero!" cried the princess, throwing her arms around him, before he'd even had a chance to get his breath back.

"I'm not a knight, I'm afraid," said Jan.

"I can see that," she said. "No horse. The main thing is, you've rescued me. Now, how are we both going to get down?"

"Don't worry," said Jan. "I'll think of something."

The River
Portugal

All her life, for as long as she could remember, they'd been on the move. Just the two of them, Joana and her father, moving from village to village, from town to town, as if they were running away.

"Why?" Joana asked him. "What are you so afraid of?"

"Of the young man who's going to steal you away from me some day."

"What young man? There's no young man."

"There will be if we don't keep moving on."

Sometimes they put down roots for a while, but if Joana was five minutes late coming home from the market, or if the old man saw a young man so much as look her way, then it was time to move on.

"What if she does find a sweetheart?" an old woman said to him. "What if she does marry him? You wouldn't be losing a daughter, you'd be gaining a son."

"Don't you want grandchildren?" another one said.

The old man only shook his head and walked away.

"Think of Joana!" the old women called after him.

"What will she do when you're dead and gone? She'll be all alone in a world full of strangers."

Next morning he was up before dawn with their bags packed, ready to be on the road again at first light.

So on they went, and on again, away from the towns and villages, up into the wild, lonely

places, till one day they stopped to rest beside
a clear mountain stream.

As Joana bent to take a drink, she saw
not her own face reflected in the water, but a
handsome young man with laughing eyes.

She started back and looked all around to
see who'd been staring over her shoulder, but
there was no one there.

When she looked again into the water he
was still there. And in the sound of the stream
tumbling over the pebbles she seemed to hear
a voice saying, "Drink, Joana. Drink."

So she scooped up the water to drink and
the touch of it on her lips was like a kiss and
the taste of it was as sweet as wild strawberries.

All next day they followed the stream down
toward the valley. All day Joana could hear
his voice in the sound of the water and the
wind sighing in the reeds. Sometimes she gave
a little skip out of pure happiness. Often and
often she bent and scooped up a handful of
water to drink.

The old man had the strangest impression
that there was a third person walking beside

them but there was no one there, only ever the mountain stream, laughing and tumbling over the pebbles.

Overnight they stopped again and in the morning Joana said, "This is a good place. Let's stay here."

The old man wouldn't hear of it.

So on they went and on again, down toward the valley.

Each day the stream grew wider, deeper till it became a river. Each day its call was louder, stronger.

"Joana! Stay with me. Don't go."

"Where are we going?" asked Joana.

"Down to the sea," said her father. "Then over the sea to some foreign place where nobody speaks our language. It will be just you and me."

"Stay with me," the river begged.

"Come with us," she said.

"The moment I touch salt water I shall be scattered into a million drops, but I'll do it for you, Joana."

"No! I won't let you."

Next morning when the old man woke, there was no sign of his daughter. He searched for her all around, "Joana! Joana!"

But there was only the song of the river for answer, sounding strangely like two voices in harmony.

"Joana! Joana!"

Calling and searching, he made his way down to the town. The people there were kind.

"She's wandered off, that's all," they said.

"Lost her way, most like, in the dark."

"She'll be back."

"One way or another—" meaning alive or dead, drowned, most likely, though they didn't like to say so—"she'll turn up."

"She'll be back," the old man told himself. He bought himself a little house close by the river and settled down to wait.

And the neighbors were kind. The women brought him puddings and pies. The men began stopping by for a chat. The children were shy at first but before very long they were playing in and out of the house.

The song of the river was the first thing he heard each morning. Why that should remind him of his lost daughter, he couldn't say, only that she'd loved the river. Half-waking, half-sleeping, he sometimes fancied he could hear her voice.

And at night the river lulled him to sleep, sounding strangely like two voices singing in harmony, one a man's voice, gentle and deep, the other a woman's, soft and sweet.

The Voice of Death
Romania

There was a man who had everything a man could want. A lovely wife and three fine children. A beautiful house and enough money to live on without lifting a finger again his whole life long. But he wasn't happy. He was so afraid of losing it all on the day he died.

"Maybe what's waiting for us in the next world is much, much better than anything here!" said his wife.

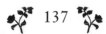

"And maybe it's not," he said. "I'm not taking any chances. I won't die if I can help it."

He packed his bags, took some of the money, left his lovely wife and his three fine children and his beautiful house, and set out, wandering through the wide world, in search of a place where nobody knew the meaning of death.

In the end he seemed to have found it.

"What's death?" they said. "No. Nobody dies here."

"So why are there so few old people?" he said.

"The old people? Oh, they move on. They hear a voice calling them and off they go."

"Where do they go?"

"To a better place."

I've heard that one before! he thought to himself. *That's the voice of Death they hear, and off they go, the fools! So all I have to do when I hear the voice of Death calling me is simply not go and I shall live forever.*

So he sent for his wife and children and they settled down to live in that place.

All went well until one day his wife suddenly stopped in the middle of cooking dinner and lifted up her head. "I hear you!" she said, snatching up her shawl. "I'm coming."

"You're not!" he said. "You're staying here."

"I must go," she said. And she ran to the door.

He caught hold of her shawl but she wriggled out of it.

Before he could bar the door, she was out of the house and away.

And was never seen again.

"Silly woman!" he said. "Didn't I warn her often enough? Didn't she know it was the voice of Death calling her? Still she went!"

Months went by and years, till one day our man was sitting in the barber's shop waiting to have his beard trimmed when he suddenly sat up straight, listening.

"I hear you!" he said. "But I'm not coming. Did you hear what I said? I'm not coming!"

He pressed his hands over his ears, but he could still hear Death calling his name.

He grabbed a handful of the barber's cotton balls and stuffed them into his ears,

but the voice had already wormed its way inside his head.

"I'm not coming!" he cried. "I'm not coming!"

Still the voice kept calling him, a siren-song of longing and forgotten dreams.

He grabbed the barber's razor out of his hand. "Right!" he said. "I'm going to fix you, Death, once and for all!"

So saying, he ran out of the door, closely followed by the barber who was naturally loath to part with his trusty razor.

Out of the town they ran, our man with the barber close on his heels, across the fields and out into the open countryside. A few of the customers joined the chase to begin with, but they soon ran out of puff and stood holding their sides, gasping for air, watching the two of them till they were out of sight.

Only the barber was there to see our man— still with the razor in his hand—go tumbling headlong into a ravine so deep and dark the barber couldn't see the bottom.

So this is where they all go, thought the

 140

barber, *when that voice he called Death calls out to them.* He hurried back to the town and fetched everyone else so they could see for themselves.

But when they got to the place, they found no ravine; only an endless, featureless plain which looked as if it had been there since time began.

And from that day on the people in that town began to die the same way as people the world over.

Violets in January

Slovakia

Poor Marusa. When her father was there, her stepmother was all sweetness and kisses. The rest of the time she treated Marusa worse than a slave. She had to do all the work around the house and if a thing wasn't done just so, her stepmother beat her. But she'd never demanded the impossible, not till one cold, winter's day when she suddenly said, "Violets! That's what this place needs to brighten it up."

 142

Without a chance to so much as snatch up a shawl, never mind argue, Marusa found herself outside on the doorstep. "And don't you dare come back," said the stepmother, "until you've found some!"

Poor Marusa! What could she do? Maybe, by some miracle, she might find a few early violets amongst the January snow. On she trudged, cold and weary, till she came to a cave where a tall, gray stone stood sentinel.

She stepped toward the cave, thinking to shelter there for a while: "Go home, child," the stone said.

And she saw it wasn't a stone at all but an old, gray man—gray beard, gray hair, twinkling gray eyes, and a gray cloak wrapped about him.

"I daren't go home," she said, "until I've found some violets for my stepmother."

"Violets? In January?"

"I know," sighed Marusa. "It's impossible."

"I wouldn't say that. But come in, child. Come in, out of the cold." He led her into the warm, dry cave, where all around people lay sleeping.

"Sister April!" the old man called.

One of the sleeping bodies stirred and slowly sat up, rubbing the sleep from her eyes. "Is it time already?"

"Not yet, sister. But here's a child with a favor to ask. Do you think you could manage a few violets out of season?"

"Violets? Of course." The young woman waved her hand and violets sprang out of the rocky floor.

"Pick them quickly," the old man said, "before she falls asleep again."

"Thank you! Thank you!" cried Marusa. Home she ran, her arms full of sweet-smelling violets.

Was the stepmother pleased? All she said was, "What took you so long?"

"Do I smell violets?" her father exclaimed when he came home next day. "Violets in

 144

January! Remarkable!"

"I thought you'd like them," the stepmother simpered. "I went to a lot of trouble."

Marusa said nothing. Let her stepmother take the credit if it kept her sweet.

Not for long. "Strawberries!" she said, right out of the blue, only a few days later. "I fancy strawberries for supper."

"Strawberries, stepmother?"

"Strawberries I said. Strawberries I will have!" So there was Marusa, locked outside in the snow again and nowhere to go for help unless the old man and his sister could work another miracle.

It wasn't his sister April he called for this time, but Cousin June.

"Strawberries?" she exclaimed. "You woke me up to ask for strawberries in January?"

"They're not for me," said Marusa, "they're for my stepmother."

"She daren't go back without them," said the old, gray man.

"Soft-hearted, that's your trouble, January," said June.

"Are you saying she can't have them?"

"Of course she shall have them!"

Was the stepmother pleased with the strawberries? If she was she didn't say so.

"Strawberries in January!" exclaimed the father when he came home. "You're a wonder, my darling!" he said, hugging the stepmother. "You know what I really miss, though, at this time of year?" Marusa's heart sank. "It's the taste of fresh apples."

"If you can find violets and strawberries in January, Marusa," the stepmother said next morning, "you can find apples too."

"Please, sir," Marusa said timidly when she stood at the mouth of the cave again.

It was a long time before old January answered. "Oh, it's you, Marusa."

"I'm sorry to trouble you again."

"You're no trouble. I'm tired, that's all. My time is almost over for another year."

"Poor old January!" said Marusa. "Standing out here in the cold and snow."

"It's of my own making."

"But I know you have a warm heart."

 146

"What has she sent you for this time?"

"Just a few apples."

"We'd better make haste and find you some. September! Wake up, you slugabed!"

September, rosy-cheeked and with tousled hair, roused himself just long enough to toss Marusa a single apple before he snuggled down to sleep again.

"Just one?" said Marusa.

"Tell your stepmother if she wants any more, she must come herself," answered January.

"Just one?" screamed the stepmother. "Was that all you brought?"

"It was all I could get," said Marusa, ducking out of the way of her stepmother's fists. "He said you can have more, but you must come yourself for them."

"Did he indeed!"

Oh, but strawberries in January! she thought. *Fresh apples, too.* What other goodies might she find simply by following Marusa's footsteps in the snow?

Wrapping her fur-trimmed cloak around

her, off she went. Soon afterward it began to snow again, lightly at first, then harder and harder, till Marusa's footprints had quite disappeared.

The stepmother struggled on through the snowstorm. On she went . . . and on . . . and on . . .

Marusa cleaned the house, fed the pigs and the chickens, milked the cow, cooked the dinner, and ate her share.

When she went to bed she left a light shining in the window to guide her stepmother home again. But the stepmother didn't come home.

Morning came and with it Marusa's father. He went straight out again to search for the stepmother. Not one trace of her did he find, not that day, nor any other day, even after the snow had melted.

Marusa went on doing on all the cooking and cleaning and looking after the animals, just as she'd done when her stepmother was there (though her father never knew it). So it wasn't long before he hardly missed the

 148

stepmother at all. To tell the truth, life was a lot more peaceful without her.

And Marusa was happy.

The Most
Beautiful Flower
Slovenia

Imagine a country where there were no old
people. No grannies knitting oversized
sweaters, baking mouth-wateringly
fattening cakes, or keeping an eye on the
grandchildren while they play. No old men
pottering in gardens or setting the world to
rights over a game of chess or backgammon
outside the local cafes.

 150

A sad place that would be. But so it was in a land not a million miles away where lived a princess so beautiful and so afraid of losing her looks that she couldn't bear old people coming near her. As if old age was catching! So she persuaded her father, the king—silly man—to banish all the old people from the kingdom.

Off they went, taking no more than they could carry or push before them in a handcart. What—all of them? Yes, all . . . bar one.

"I'm not letting you go, Grandpa," said Johan. "How can I run the farm without you? There's still so much I don't know and you do. Anyway, I like having you around."

"You'll get us both into trouble," the old man said.

"Only if they find you."

That they never did. After one mug of the old man's home-brewed beer, the king's spies couldn't be bothered to take a proper look around.

Meanwhile, back in the palace . . .

The king loved his daughter very much. But not so much that he didn't realize she'd need

a wise man for a husband to help her rule the kingdom after he was dead and gone.

There was no shortage of candidates. So the king said there would be a competition. A test of fine judgment and quick thinking. The first to announce the very moment of sunrise on Midsummer's Day would win the princess's hand in marriage.

Well before dawn they were all lined up, eyes fixed on the eastern horizon. Except for Johan who stood facing the other way, toward the mountains in the west.

The other young men—knights, nobles, army officers, and rich merchants' sons— nudged one another and smirked. What a fool! What a clodhopper! Didn't he know the sun always rose in the east?

Not long now. Dawn was approaching. Some of them, afraid of missing their chance, cried out, "Now!" too soon and were disqualified.

When Johan shouted, "Now!" there were smirks and nudges all around again, until they saw the sun just peeping above the

eastern horizon. He'd picked the moment exactly right.

"Well done!" said the king. "But how did you do it?"

"The moment the sunlight strikes the mountain tops in the west," said Johan, "is the moment before the sun rises in the east."

The king smiled; this was the very son-in-law he was looking for. But the princess was looking Johan up and down; at his muddy boots and homespun clothes. His ruddy cheeks and tousled hair. She'd no intention of marrying a common farm boy! She whispered in her father's ear.

The king shook his head, but maybe she was right. Maybe it was just a lucky chance after all that Johan had called out at just the right moment. So he announced another competition. The man clever enough to work out how to come to the palace next day wearing shoes but barefoot, he would be the one to marry the princess.

That was a sight to see! Some of the suitors came with one shoe off and one shoe on. Some came in sandals without socks. Some just turned up in their socks. A few came with shoes painted onto their bare feet.

Only Johan seemed to have turned up in the same old pair of muddy old boots as yesterday, until he turned up his feet to show the king that the boots had no soles!

The king laughed. "Well done!" he said and was about to proclaim him the winner when the princess tugged at his sleeve. "You said shoes," she said. "He's supposed to be wearing shoes but barefoot. But he's not wearing shoes, he's wearing boots!"

The king sighed and shook his head.

"This time I shall choose!" said the princess. "The man who brings me the flower that is most like me, he is the one I shall marry!"

Next morning the palace courtyard was like a cross between a florist's shop and a

funeral. Flowers everywhere! Roses, lilies, and carnations. Orchids, pansies, honeysuckle, orange blossom—you name it. And Johan with an armful of ripe corn.

The princess stamped her foot and screamed at him, "How could you? Corn isn't even a flower!"

"Corn is more beautiful than any flower," said Johan. "And so are you. Flowers fade and wither, but corn grows even more beautiful as it ages. When the corn is ripe we harvest it to make bread. Without bread, we'd all die. I'm not saying that without your love I'd die—"

"Then don't!" snapped the princess.

"Come with me, then," said Johan, "and I'll show you a field of ripe corn the same color as your hair."

"That's better," said the princess. "And are my lips the color of the poppies that grow among the corn? And are my eyes as blue as cornflowers?"

"Come and see!"

So she came to the farm and she saw the ripe corn swaying in the wind. The poppies

and the cornflowers.

"Now I'll show you the man you should be marrying," said Johan. "The one who solved your father's riddles."

When the princess set eyes on Johan's grandfather, she gave a little cry and would have fainted clean away if Johan hadn't held her upright.

"Banish my grandfather," he whispered, "and I'll go with him. Or else let him stay and let the others come back. He gets lonely, you know, with no one his own age to talk to. So, let them come back. We could issue the proclamation on our wedding day."

"Why, so we could!" said the princess.

And so they did.

Half-Chick
Spain

H alf-chick was born with only one eye, one wing, and one leg, but his mother loved him more than all her other chicks put together.

"Half-chick's special," she said. "Half-chick is destined for great things. One day the whole world will look up to him."

"I'm Half-chick!" cheeped Half-chick. "Mama says I'm destined for great things. One day the whole world will look up to me."

Till his brothers and sisters got sick of him carrying on and pushed him out into the farmyard.

Half-chick picked himself up and dusted himself off. "I'm Half-chick. I'm special," he told the ducks, the pigs, the goats, the sheep, as he hopped around the farmyard.

None of them took any notice.

"One day the whole world will look up to me!" crowed Half-chick.

The big old world just kept on turning.

So off went Half-chick, out of the farmyard, hopping down the lane, till he came to a stream so choked with weeds it was no more than a trickle.

"Help me!" cried the stream. "Clear just a few of these weeds out of the way or I shall die."

"Help you?" said Half-chick. "I've got no time to help you. I'm Half-chick. I'm special. One day the whole world will look up to me!"

On he went until he came to a dying bonfire.

"Help me!" cried the fire. "Throw a stick or two on me before I go out."

"Help you?" said Half-chick. "I've got no

158

time to help you. I'm Half-chick. One day the whole world will look up to me!"

On he went again until he came to a tree with the wind trapped in its branches.

"Help me!" sighed the wind. "Just shake the branches a little and I shall be free."

"Help you?" said Half-chick. "I've got no time to help you. I'm Half-chick. I'm special. I'm destined for great things. One day the whole world will look up to me."

So on he hopped and on again until he came to the town. He was tired now and hungry. From an open kitchen window he smelt the most delicious smell.

He hopped up onto the windowsill so he could smell it better.

Next thing he knew he was tumbling straight into the stewpot simmering on the stove.

"Help!" he cried. "Help me! I'm drowning."

"Help you?" bubbled the water. "Why should I help you? You didn't help my brother when he was choking."

"Help!" cried Half-chick again. "I'm boiling!"

"Help you?" said the fire. "Why should I help you? You wouldn't help my cousin when he was dying."

"Won't somebody help me?" cried Half-chick. Whether the cook heard him or not, it was the cook who saved him. Picked him up and tossed him out of the window where the wind caught him up, spun him around, and carried him higher and higher.

It set him down at last on the topmost point of the church spire.

"And there you can stay!" said the wind.

And there he did stay. And people did look up to him and they still do, whenever they want to know which way the wind is blowing.

"Look at me!" he crows, spinning round and round on his one leg. "Look at me! I'm Half-chick! I'm on top of the world!"

Lars, My Lad!
Sweden

There was a young man who went wandering through the world to seek his fortune. Footsore and weary and with night closing in, he came to a lonely cottage. He knocked at the door but no one answered. So in he went and found the place empty, nothing but a great brass-bound trunk standing in the middle of the floor.

Naturally he opened it—wouldn't you?— and looked inside.

The trunk was empty, but for a scrap of old parchment.

He held the parchment up to the dying light from the window and read aloud the words written there: "Lars, my lad!"

"What is your wish, master?" said a voice, soft as the rustle of the wind through autumn leaves.

He looked around. There was no one there.

He read the words again: "Lars, my lad!"

"What is your wish, master?"

"What is my wish? It's for a good hot meal and a glass of ale."

In the blink of an eye, there was a table, set ready for dinner, the food piping hot and a glass of ale to wash it down.

He made short work of that. Then he took out the parchment again. "Lars, my lad!"

"What is your wish, master?"

"A soft feather bed and a good night's sleep."

A soft feather bed he had, but a good night's sleep was harder to come by; was this a case of three wishes and no more? If so, he must be very careful not to waste his third wish.

Next morning—"Lars, my lad!"

"What is your wish, master?"

"I'd like a place of my own where I can settle down. A house—no, make that a palace, with a few acres—make that square miles—of land."

There he was, master of a grand house and a landowner—but so shabbily dressed!

Three wishes he'd had, but where was the harm in asking for more? "Lars, my lad! I need a new suit of clothes—several new suits—a wardrobe full!"

And there were the clothes, all hanging in a row!

He could have anything in the world he wanted—Persian carpets and silks from China. All he had to say was, "Lars, my lad!"

Meanwhile, not far down the road, on the other side of the forest, the King rose from his bed, strolled onto the battlements to survey his kingdom; stopped; looked; rubbed his eyes and looked again.

Was that a palace over there? It wasn't there yesterday, was it?

"Was it?" he asked the princess, his daughter.

"I've never noticed it before," she said. "I wonder who it belongs to. Let's ride over and take a look."

So they rode through the forest and came to the young man's palace and found a sumptuous feast—"Lars, my lad!"—laid out to greet them. After which the king felt it was hardly polite to ask who the young man was and how come his palace had sprung up overnight. As for the princess, she was quite bowled over by the Persian carpets and the Chinese silk hangings—it was all so different from her father's draughty old castle. The owner was not bad-looking and before they left he gave her a necklace of pearls from the Indies.

To cut a long story short, they were married.

In the wee small hours of his wedding night the young man was woken by a voice soft as the rustle of the wind through dry leaves.

"Master! Master! What is your wish, master?"

"Nothing," the young man murmured. "I've got everything in the world I could possibly want."

"Then set me free, master. Give me that piece of parchment you found in that old brass-bound trunk."

So the young man gave him the parchment and settled down to sleep again.

In the morning—what a shock for the princess! She was lying on the cold, hard ground in an empty cottage. Off she went, home to her father, in floods of tears.

Before he was properly awake, the young man found himself in the stocks, for people to jeer at and throw things at till evening came and they all went home.

There was no one left, save a creature so wizened he might have been as old as the hills, and yet no bigger than a child. Beside him stood a barrow piled high with worn-out shoes and boots.

"Serves you right!" he crowed. "Serves you right! See all these, on my barrow? These are the shoes and boots I've worn out fetching and carrying for you!"

"Lars, my lad?"

"That's me! And this is the bit of parchment that gave you power over me!"

"This?" said the young man, grabbing it as it was waved under his nose. "Lars, my lad!"

The creature screamed in fury. "What is your wish, master?" he groaned.

"To have everything back as it was this time yesterday."

And so it was, right down to the king and the princess having no memory of anything being amiss.

Since he did now have everything he could possibly wish for, the young man took the parchment and hid it in a secret place where no one, including Lars, my lad, would ever find it. Though there are those who are still looking.

Tam Lin
United Kingdom

First they were children together. Then they were sweethearts together. And everyone was thinking it wouldn't be long before Tam Lin and Burd Janet were happy-ever-aftering together when Tam Lin disappeared.

Long after all their neighbors had given him up for dead, Burd Janet went on searching for him, over the fields and hills while summer turned to autumn. Through the wild wood

she wandered, searching, always searching, picking flowers as she went, weaving them into a garland for her hair.

"And what is the point of putting flowers in your hair, Burd Janet," she sighed to her own reflection in a woodland pool, "if Tam Lin isn't here to see you?"

"But I *can* see you," a voice whispered.

"Tam Lin!" She started up, looking all around, but there was no one there. "Tam Lin! Where are you?"

"Not here."

"Then where?"

"In Elfland. It was the Queen of Elfland who carried me off as I lay sleeping among the hollow hills."

"What is it like—Elfland?"

"It is a place without pain or sorrow, old age or death, and I would be happy to stay here if you were with me."

"Then I will come to you."

"The Queen will not let you."

"Then come back to me, Tam Lin!"

"I cannot do it without your help. But it will be a hard thing for you to do."

"It cannot be harder than living my whole life long without you."

"Well, then, tomorrow is All Hallows Eve when the ghosts of dead men rise from their graves to walk among the living and witches ride the wind. Good people bolt their doors and keep the fire burning bright till morning. Do you dare come back to this place alone at midnight with your green cloak wrapped about you?"

"I dare."

"Then you shall see the Queen of Elfland come riding by with all her court following after and I shall be at the queen's right hand. Drag me from my horse and hold me fast. Whatever happens you must not let me go till I stand before you in my own, true shape, or I shall be lost for ever."

So there she stood on All Hallows Eve with her green cloak wrapped about her and saw the Queen of Elfland come riding with all

her court following after and Tam Lin riding beside her.

Then Janet leaped up and dragged him from the saddle and held him tight, while the elf-crew shrieked and howled about her.

Then it was a slithery eel she was holding in her arms, but she held it fast, knowing it was Tam Lin.

The eel turned into a venomous snake, but still she held it, knowing Tam Lin would do her no harm.

The snake reared up and became a swan, its great wings thrashing. Then it was a dove and she was afraid of crushing the life out of it and almost let it flutter free.

Through all these changes she held fast, knowing it was her own Tam Lin and if she lost him now it would be forever. Even when he was turned to a block of ice that almost froze her to the heart, and when the ice was turned to fire and she felt her hair singed and her face scorched and felt her own flesh burning, still she held him, until the fire dwindled into a bar of red-hot iron.

So it remained for longer than any mortal flesh could bear but still she bore it until, half-fainting, she flung herself, still clutching the bar of red-hot iron, into the forest pool.

The water bubbled and hissed. Steam rose all about her and as it cleared, she saw it was her own Tam Lin she was holding in her arms.

Burd Janet wrapped her green cloak around them both and held him tight while the elf-crew howled and screamed about them and the Queen of Elfland wept bitter tears. "Oh, Tam Lin!" she cried. "I should have plucked out your eyes! I should have cut out your human heart and given you a heart of stone! I never thought a mortal woman could steal you away from me and all that I can give you. Marry her, then! Know sorrow and pain. Grow old together and then die!"

With that she rode away and all the troops of Elfland after her.

Burd Janet was married to Tam Lin and they lived until they died. They had their

 171

share of mortal sorrow and pain. But there was happiness too, and laughter. These too are things that the elf-kind will never know.

Afterword

Since the time before time began, whiling away the hours between dinner and bedtime in the flickering firelight, resting in the noonday heat, or tramping along some dusty lane, trying to find ways of making the long road seem shorter, people have always told one another stories. Merchants and pilgrims, soldiers and seasonal farmworkers and the craftsmen who worked on the great cathedrals wandered across Europe, taking their stories with them. After they'd gone, the

 173

local storytellers would try to recall the best of the tales they told, missing out a bit here and there, maybe, but then adding in some little detail of their own.

I was worried when I first set out to make this collection—just one from each country of the European Union—that I wouldn't be able to track down each story to the place where it truly belonged, the place where it was first told. The more I read, the more versions I found of the same story told in different countries hundreds of miles apart, and I came to realize it didn't matter where they began because they are all part of common European heritage.

Most, I hope, will be new to you. A few you may have heard before, but maybe not quite as I've chosen to tell them.

After you've read them, close this book and try retelling just one of the stories to your family or friends or classmates. However well you think you remember it, I guarantee it will come out differently from the way I've told it, because you'll have added a little something of your own, just as every storyteller has always done, right back to the time before time began.